THE

MINNESOTA HANDBOOK,

FOR

1856-7.

WITH A NEW AND ACCURATE MAP.

BY

NATHAN H. PARKER,

AUTHOR OF "IOWA AS IT IS," "SECTIONAL AND GEOLOGICAL MAP OF IOWA," "IOWA HANDBOOK," ETC.

BOSTON:
JOHN P. JEWETT AND COMPANY.
CLEVELAND, OHIO: H. P. B. JEWETT.
NEW YORK: SHELDON, BLAKEMAN AND COMPANY.
M DCCC LVII.

LITHOTYPED BY THE AMERICAN STEREOTYPE COMPANY,
PHŒNIX BUILDING, BOSTON.

PREFACE.

THE author of the following pages, from extensive acquaintance both East and West, perceiving a great want of reliable information on the Territory of Minnesota and her resources, has, by extended tours through various portions of the Territory, by careful observation and frequent inquiry, placed himself in possession of information which enables him to present in this work a true exposition of the resources, the climate, the soil, the condition of cities, towns, and villages, and the actual settlement and present condition of this growing Territory, which, though organized but six years ago, now possesses the requisite population to enable her to knock at the door of the Union for admission as a State!

To place this information within the reach of all who may be directing their attention to this Territory, he has decided to condense this information into as brief space as possible, thus giving it to the public in the form of this Handbook, to be revised from year to year, intending as soon as practicable to place before the public a larger and more extensive work on Minnesota.

To the capitalist, seeking a field for investment; to the traveler, seeking those scenes of beauty that lie spread out with that lavishness that nature seldom exhibits; to the immigrant, seeking a home among these fertile vales and pebbly streams, this little book is respectfully dedicated. That prosperity and success may attend them, through the development of the resources of this great Territory, is the sincere desire of the author.

NATHAN H. PARKER.

September 1, 1856.

CONTENTS.

CHAPTER V.

CHAPTER VI.

CHAPTER VII.

CHAPTER VIII.

CHAPTER IX.

CHAPTER X.

CHAPTER XI.

CHAPTER XII.

CHAPTER XIII.

CHAPTER XIV.

CHAPTER XV.

CHAPTER XVI.

CHAPTER XVII.

CHAPTER XVIII.

CHAPTER XIX.

CHAPTER XX.

CHAPTER XXI.

MINNESOTA HANDBOOK.

CHAPTER I.

THE UPPER MISSISSIPPI.

On one of the pleasant mornings in early June, I found myself a passenger on the Northern Bell, Capt. Preston Lodwick, and clerks De Bois and Cooley, in command, with a full trip of passengers on board, bound for Minnesota. This is the season when pleasure-seekers from the crowded East or the sunny South seek a retreat from care and toil, on the shaded, pebbly shores of the crystal lakes, or by the foaming torrent of the cataract, intent upon enjoying to the utmost the numerous advantages afforded by the northwest to those in quest of health, wealth, or pleasure.

At this season of the year, every thoroughfare leading to the West and Northwest is thronged, and at times the boats passing up the river are crowded to their utmost capacity. The writer was one of five hundred who made the trip to Minnesota early in the spring, on one of the Minnesota packets. State-rooms were entirely out of the question, and bunks upon the floor or seats at the table were at a premium. Standing at the lower end of the cabin, and gazing upon the hundreds of persons whose beds covered almost every foot of the cabin floor, I intuitively exclaimed, "This is going west." I mused upon the various situations and climates and nations these people had left; the misfortunes that had befallen some, and the fortunes that had fallen to others, alike impelling them to seek the "land of promise — the great West," each individual having different plans and anticipations for the future, and each seeming to delight in being one of this hurly-burly, motley throng.

The conclusion that I came to, was, that whoever finds himself in possession of a state-room, and in the enjoyment of all the comforts and luxuries found on board the floating palaces of the upper Mississippi, may consider himself highly favored.

This is the season when all nature is gay, when the hills and dells are robed in their fullest foliage; and nowhere on this continent can be found scenery more grand and romantic and interesting than upon the upper Mississippi. The hills and bluffs and slopes, now precipitous and rugged, presenting a castellated front of rock from two to five hundred feet high, almost overhanging the water, again sloping gracefully down to the water's edge, bedecked here and there with clusters of small oak trees and flowers of almost every variety and hue, extend along the river on either shore for a hundred miles or more, and are as various as extensive. Many of these bluffs are but the termini or projecting promontory of a succession of equally high and beautiful bluffs, similar in character, but of every conceivable shape and size, stretching away up the valleys of some tributary stream, and from which, again, diverge other ranges of bluffs and hills, on the banks of its tributaries, which hills are smaller in size but no less beautiful.

The range of bluffs along either shore of the river are from two to four miles apart. The river meanders along this valley, now washing the base of the beetling cliffs on the eastern shore, for miles, while those on the opposite side are seen towering up high above the woodland in the valley intervening; again it divides itself into numerous channels, forming thousands of beautiful islands clad in densest foliage; and yet again it winds its way to the western shore, bathing the feet of the beautiful bluffs and sloping hills, rounded with taste and skill such as no art of man can imitate, and set out with trees, here and there, gracefully arranged like orchards, and covered with grass and flowers to their very summits.

On the river below Dubuque or above St. Paul, or a few miles east or west from the river at any point, you reach the beautiful and fertile prairies.

The first idea that will impress itself upon the observer is, that "these prairies have been cleared by the patient labor of another race of men, removing all the forests, and roots, and stumps, and brambles, and smoothing them down as with mighty rollers, and sowing them with grass and flowers; a race which then passed away, having built no houses of their own, and made no fences, and established no landmarks to lay the foundation of any future claim." The mounds which you here and there see, look, indeed, as if a portion of this unknown race had died, and had been buried there, and left these as memorials of their presence. Whence came this people, and whither have they departed?

"Are they here —
The dead of other days? And did the dust
Of these fair solitudes once stir with life,
And burn with passion? Let the mighty mounds
That overlook the rivers, or that rise
In the dim forest, crowded with old oaks,
Answer. A race that long has passed away
Built them! A disciplined and populous race
Heaped, with long toil, the earth, while yet the Greek
Was hewing the Pentelicus to forms
Of symmetry, and rearing on its rock
The glittering Parthenon. These ample fields
Nourish'd their harvests; here their herds were fed,
When haply by their stalls the bison low'd
And bow'd his maned shoulder to the yoke.
All day this desert murmured with their toils,
Till twilight blush'd and lovers walk'd and woo'd
In a forgotten language, and old tunes,
From instruments of unremember'd form,

Gave the soft winds a voice. The red man came—
The roaming hunter tribes, warlike and fierce,
And the mound-builders vanish'd from the earth.
The solitude of centuries untold
Has settled where they dwelt. The prairie wolf
Howls in their meadows, and his fresh dug den
Yawns by my path. The gopher mines the ground
Where stood their swarming cities. All is gone—
All! save the piles of earth that hold their bones,
The platforms where they worshipp'd unknown gods."

We live not in a *new* world. "Not a foot of ground that we tread but has been trod before us." Dahkota and Ojibway, Shianu and Ausinabwaun, Winnebago and Ioway, Ozaukie and Musquakie, have each, together or in succession, dwelt in this land, hunted and warred through it, migrated to and from it; and now the Anglo-Saxon race, following the "Star of Empire" as their "star in the West," have taken possession of these magnificently beautiful and unsurpassably fertile fields.

But I digress—my object is not to write the past history, but the present condition and future prospects, of Minnesota Territory.

The geographical limits of Minnesota, as defined by act of Congress, extend from the Mississippi and St. Croix Rivers and the western extremity of Lake Superior on the east, to the Missouri and White Earth Rivers on the west; and from the Iowa line on the south, to the boundary line between the United States and the British possessions on the north. The Territory comprises an

2

area of one hundred and sixty-six thousand square miles, or one hundred and six millions of acres; lying between parallels 43° 30′ and 49° of north latitude, and extending between 90 and 103° of west longitude. The Territorial Government of Minnesota was established by an act of Congress, approved 3rd of March, 1849.

CHAPTER II.

UPPER MISSISSIPPI TOWNS. — THEIR CONDITION AND PROSPECTS.

Brownsville, the county-seat of Houston county, is the first point in the Territory, passing up the Mississippi. It is situated at the mouth of Wild Cat Creek, and one hundred and fifty-three miles above Dubuque. The United States land office, formerly located at this place, has been removed to Chatfield, some sixty miles distant, in Fillmore county.

The next point above is La Crosse, Wisconsin, a city of probably 4000 inhabitants, and growing very rapidly. This city is to be the terminus of two railroad lines, each of which are being pushed westward with energy. The earnings of sixty-one miles now completed of the La Crosse and Milwaukie Railroad, for June last, were upwards of $50,000. La Crosse is, and will doubtless continue to be, the most important river point in Wisconsin.

La Crescent, directly opposite La Crosse, is a town recently laid out, which promises to be a place of much importance, and the commercial emporium of Houston and adjoining interior counties. The town is situated at the mouth of Hokah or Root River, which stream takes its rise in Mower and Olmstead counties, some seventy-five miles distant. A company has been organized who are preparing for the continuation of the La Crosse and Milwaukie Railroad, westward from La Crescent, up the valley of Root River to South Bend on the Minnesota River. Hon. Thomas B. Stoddard, mayor of La Crosse, is president of this company. This site is in the hands of J. T. Boyle, of Danville, Ky., J. M. Bryant, of La Crescent, and others; who, we understand, will this fall and next spring erect a large hotel, and such manufactories and buildings as this rapidly growing town and the rich agricultural country in rear of it may demand.

Winona, the county-seat of Winona county, is situated forty miles above La Crosse, and one hundred and fifty below St. Paul. The traveller will seldom find anywhere more grand and imposing scenery than that surrounding Winona. The town is situated upon a beautiful level prairie, several miles in extent, surrounded by high and rugged promontories, in places almost overhanging the plain below. Five beautiful valleys converge on to this delightful plain—the White Water, Rolling Stone, Gilmore, Burns', and Pleasant valleys—each bounded on either side by a range of bluffs, stretching away back into the interior, with hills and moles of every conceivable shape. The country interior is rapidly filling up, and the natural roads, leading out to the numerous new towns in rear of Winona, contribute to make it an important river town. This place is but three years old, and the titles to the land upon which the town stands were not perfected until October last; yet, with all the obstacles, it has grown to contain at present a population of upwards of 2500! The town-site, with additions, contains eight hundred acres, divided into two thousand five hundred lots, which are selling at prices varying from $100 to $4000. The U. S. land office, a three-story banking and land agency house, a steam saw-mill, and a large, first-class hotel, are among the principal public buildings recently erected. A court-house and jail, of stone, to cost $10,000, and two additional saw-mills, are under contract.

Winneiska, eighteen miles above Winona, at the mouth of the Whitewater River, is a new town, with much thrift and energy, and the landing for a large section of country.

Wabashaw, twenty-five miles farther up, is a thrifty young town.

Reid's Landing, five miles above, and two miles below the foot of Lake Pepin, contains seventy buildings, and is an important river landing.

Lake Pepin is a beautiful sheet of water, twenty-five miles long by an average width of five miles. The bluffs are very rugged and precipitous on either shore, and the distance between them does not seem to differ much from the space between them for a hundred miles below, and "it would seem that the lake was made by weeding out the islands, and thus leaving the base of bluffs to be bathed by the Father of Waters."

The bluffs here, on either shore, are rugged and precipitous. At the great bend of this lake, on the northeast side, is a conspicuous escarpment, celebrated in Indian annals as the Maiden's Rock, or Cap des Sioux. From this rock, tradition informs us that "Winona, the beautiful daughter of an Indian chief, precipated herself rather than to marry a man she did not love. She illustrated some of the noblest principles of our nature, and hence her name is immortal, while fashionable belles by the thousand pass away and are forgotten forever."

The Maiden's Rock is four hundred and ten feet high—the perpendicular wall of lower magnesian limestone being nearly two hundred feet. Lake Pepin, near its mouth, has been sounded four hundred fathoms without finding bottom.

Lake City, Central Point, and Florence, are within three miles of each other, on the west bank of Lake Pepin, on one of the most beautiful plains in the western country. The high, picturesque bluffs that have hugged either shore so long, above and below, here stretch back, leaving a level plateau containing probably ten thousand acres, dotted here and there with small lakes of clear pure water, and groves of medium-sized trees. This plain is eight miles long on the lake and three to four miles wide in the centre, bounded on the west by a range of high, thickly wooded bluffs, and on the east by the lake — a desirable spot for a large rural village, or watering-place, or even for farming purposes. This land is upon the Half-breed Reservation, which accounts for the slow growth of these three embryotic towns.

The shores of Lake Pepin, and of the river, for twenty miles above, are lined with an immense number of logs, and two or three steamers are constantly employed in towing rafts of logs and of lumber from the booms, at the head of the lake, through into the current of the river below.*

Wacouta, at the head of the lake, is a point of considerable importance to lumbermen, as here the rafts are many of them prepared for their long voyage down the river.

Red Wing, six miles above the head of the lake, is beautifully and advantageously located, and will become a point of commercial importance. This town is the county-seat of Goodhue county, and

* Red Rock, six miles below St. Paul, is a point of some note. Upon this rock certain tribes of Indians have for years laid their offerings, and a chief informs me that "no good Indian passes this rock without leaving here tobacco, wampum, beads, skins, or other valuables, as offerings to the Great Spirit." Of course, the more valuable the offering, the better the Indian.

had a population, in July, of 1500, and is rapidly improving. Here is located the Hamline University, under the auspices of the M. E. Church, attended by upwards of seventy students, with a fine brick edifice for the preparatory department, costing $10,000. This society have a beautiful site, embracing thirty acres, upon which they are preparing to erect a college building to cost $25,000. The Presbyterians are building a brick church, to be of sufficient dimensions to contain four hundred hearers. An ably conducted newspaper, and a new hotel building, forty-six by one hundred and four feet, and the U. S. land office for this district, are among the more important "public institutions" of this young city. A lot on Main street was sold, recently, for $500 in the morning, and again in the afternoon for the sum of $1,000. A part of a lot on the corner of Bush and Third streets, which last year cost about $200, was sold for $800.

Point Prescott, twenty-eight miles above Red Wing, on the Wisconsin shore, is a town of perhaps 800 inhabitants, and enjoys a healthy and substantial growth, has a handsome location, which is being well improved.

Point Douglas lies opposite Point Prescott, from the northwest side, on the tongue of land between the junction of the St. Croix and Mississippi. The buildings are neat and the town has a business-like appearance.

Hastings, one of the most pleasantly located and rapidly improving towns in the Territory, is situated on the west side of the river, three miles above the mouth of Lake St. Croix (Point Douglas), and twenty-five miles below St. Paul. The town site of Hastings is a naturally terraced plateau of land, shaded by a natural grove of medium-sized oak trees. At the lower end of the town, and partly included within the corporate limits, is Lake Isabel, covering an area of about eighty acres. The town plat embraces four hundred and seventy acres. This town is but fifteen months old, and contains 1500 inhabitants! Everything in and about the place seems thrifty, every body busy, hotels all full, from cellar to garret, coaches and conveyances westward constantly crowded. Hastings is the natural river-point for the fertile region of country watered by the Cannon, Straight, and Vermillion rivers, and now bids fair to become one of the largest and most important cities on the Upper Mississippi, below St. Paul.

One mile southwest from Hastings is the Vermillion River, with a fall of one hundred and fifty feet within a mile, producing a succession of cascades. Below the falls, the river passes between perpendicular walls of rock, nearly a hundred feet in height, standing two hundred feet apart. Through this chasm, the river winds its way beneath the deep dark foliage that hangs in tufts from the projecting rocks, or the tall, straight trees that stand like sentinels on either shore.

CHAPTER III.

ST. PAUL.—HER PAST, PRESENT, AND FUTURE.

St. Paul, the capitol of the Territory and seat of justice of Ramsay county, is pleasantly situated on the east bank of the Mississippi River, upon a plain some eighty feet above the river, and eight hundred feet above the Gulf of Mexico. The land now occupied by the commercial emporium of this great Territory was in part pre-empted in 1838. The town was surveyed in 1845, and as late as the spring of 1847 there were but three white families upon the ground now occupied by a city of 10,000 intelligent and industrious American citizens. To recapitulate: in 1846, St. Paul contained but ten white inhabitants; ten years afterwards, its census shows a population of 10,000! We can express our astonishment at this rapid growth, in no better terms than those used by Lieut. Maury, in his address at the celebration of the Minnesota Historical Society, at St. Paul, on the 24th of June last. We extract from his remarks:

"Where are we, and what are we doing? I find it difficult to realize the fact that I am not among enchanted spirits at work upon things of magic in some fairy land; for here, and on my way here, I have in this great valley of the West realized things, facts, and merits, which, could they have been foretold in our fathers' hearing, would have been considered by them as too extravagant and highly wrought even for a nursery tale, in which goblins and witches and fairies and magic are allowed to figure.

"There was once in dream-land a youth, who, the romancers tell us, possessed himself of a charm by which he would summon to his possession the most powerful genii, and have them do his will. Get for me, said he to the genii, jewels of silver and jewels of gold, and caskets of rubies and diamonds and precious stones; and lo! riches and wealth stood in great heaps and piles before him. Build me, said he, before the morning's sun shall gild the east, a palace more gorgeous and splendid than the king's; let it, in grandeur, surpass all other palaces that were ever built. And, in the morning, there it was, to the amazement and wonder of the king, his daughter, his princes and his nobles. We have all read these tales of entertainment in the nursery, and, in the simplicity of childhood, wondered if they were true, sure enough!

"But here, in this western world, in this blessed land of liberty, under this glorious Union, there is a people who have a charm, by which they can call up, and have called up, and are every day calling up, genii far more powerful than any that

Aladdin, with his wonderful lamp, ever dreamed of. Give us, they say in their spirit, indomitable enterprise and energy; give us not caskets of stones, but the elements of greatness, of human prosperity and happiness, and make us mighty and great; and lo! as if the wand of the great magician had touched the country, the savage and the wild beast disappear, tall trees bow their heads, and the forests fall to the ground, and in their places we behold the school-house, the church with its tall taper spire pointing heavenward, and broad fields of yellow grain waving to the breeze, and making the very hills smile and leap with plenty — making glad the hearts of freemen.

"They say to it, the creation of a place in a night is not enough for us; we want cities with gilded domes, and temples of science, and halls of learning, and splendid charities; and lo! they stand where the wilderness was but yesterday, and they rise up as if from the green bosom of your smiling prairies."

The site where St. Paul now stands, was, eight years ago, a wilderness; now a proud city of 10,000 inhabitants, possessing all the elements of refined civilization, greets the eye and astonishes every beholder. Where but a few moons ago the pale-face would have fallen a prey to the tomahawk and the scalping-knife, now stands the house of worship, with its tall spire; and instead of the war-whoop is heard the church-going bell, or the melodious voices of a hundred happy Sabbath-school children, in praise to the Great Spirit who has given them a home in this goodly land.

In a work of this size, our space is too limited to enter into details as to the number and character of the business houses of St. Paul. A city of its rapid growth, present importance, and future greatness, is of itself a subject for an entire volume. We annex, however, some statistics of trade in 1854, for which I am indebted to the Minnesota Pioneer:

	Capital invested.	Business done.
Groceries	$96,500	244,500
Groceries, dry goods, and dealers in Indian goods	152,000	550,000
Liquors	7,500	53,000
Jewelry, clocks, etc.	6,500	23,000
Hardware, Iron, etc.	43,000	85,000
Books, stationery, etc.	21,000	50,000
Dry goods	115,000	251,000
Fancy goods	4,000	15,000
Confectionery, fruits, etc.	5,000	15,000
Druggists	37,000	99,000
Furniture	8,000	41,000
Auction and commission		90,000
Tailors' and clothing establishments	59,000	148,000
Stoves, tinware, etc.	97,000	99,000
Shoe dealers and manufacturers	37,000	90,000
Saddlery and harness manufacturers and dealers in leather	8,400	28,000
Forwarding and commission merchants		489,000
Bankers		3,559,000
Express		3,158
Livery business	61,000	69,000
	$719,400	$5,868,500

"A glance at the above figures will show what St. Paul is in its mercantile capacity, and what manner of growth it has had since 1849, when its entire business amounted to about $131,000 only. From small beginnings St. Paul has grown great as rapidly as a bird unfolds its wings for an upward flight. No sudden combination of circumstances has brought about this result. It has been accomplished by hard and unremitted labor.

"A bird's eye view is given of the manufactures of St. Paul as they are now. No contrast can be made of them with 1849, for the reason that, in that year, the principal and in fact only manufacturers in St. Paul were those who wielded the axe, the hammer, and the plane—before whose sturdy strokes the forest bowed to the ground above which it had stood so grandly, and by whose industry log cabins and shanties were made to occupy the 'clearings.' A gratifying result can be shown in this department of St. Paul's wealth. The man who six years ago would have ventured to predict that there would be at this time in St. Paul steam engines driving saw-mills, sash machines, turning lathes, printing presses, etc., would have been regarded as wanting common sense in a lamentable degree; but time proves it—all of them are here; and, what is better, more and still more are coming."

Of manufactories, I noticed one mill, with machinery, driven by an engine of seventy horsepower, capable of turning out 32,000 feet lumber, 20,000 shingles, 16,000 laths, and planing, tongueing and grooving 12,000 feet of flooring every day. Beside this, there are four other mills of less capacity, but producing from five to ten thousand feet of lumber per day. There are also two grist mills, one foundry, one door, sash, and blind factory, etc. An extensive establishment for the manufacture of agricultural implements is about going into operation.

Large and substantial edifices of stone and brick are being erected, indicating that architectural taste and wealth, civilization and refinement, are here. Of the principal public buildings, mention may be made of the State House, first Presbyterian Church, Baldwin School, Court-house, public Market-house, Winslow Hotel, Santominy Hotel, and the Fuller House. The latter building is one hundred and twenty feet square, and five stories high. In addition to many business houses and dwellings, there are now in process of erection, or about to be commenced, a Catholic cathedral, a Masonic hall, a theatre, and an Odd Fellows' hall, all to be splendid buildings. The material now preparing for the cathedral indicates that it will be one of the most magnificent buildings in the West.

Some idea may be formed of the amount of travel thitherward, from the fact that the receipts of the Winslow House, the principal hotel in St. Paul, in June last were $6500, and about the same in July—averaging $6000 per month. There are twelve hotels in the city, each doing a good business! "During the past season the arriving steamboats landed upwards of forty-five thousand passengers. It is entirely safe to estimate that each of these persons left, in necessary expenses, the sum of ten dollars, and this will give an addition of $450,000 to the currency of the place."

CHAPTER IV.

THE SIGHT-SEER'S DIURNAL DRIVE.

To those who have but a day or two to spend in sight-seeing in Minnesota, I will mention the most advantageous route. Procure, at one of the livery stables in St. Paul, early in the morning, a conveyance suited to the number in company; then proceed, via St. Anthony, to Cheever's observatory in St. Anthony City, about half a mile below, yet in full view of the Falls of St. Anthony. This tower is about one hundred feet high, and affords an unsurpassed view of the rapids and cataract, of the beautiful cities of St. Anthony and Minneapolis, and of the wire suspension bridge, spanning the Father of Waters, between them; also, a view of an immense extent of country in every direction, forming "one of the most charming and extensive landscapes in Minnesota." This observatory is safe, and you need but follow the rules — "pay your dime and climb."

Thence you continue up to the Falls of St. Anthony. Here you are upon the Niagara of the northwest, first discovered by Hennepin in 1680, and now the object of admiration for thousands of visitors who throng its banks annually. (See full description on another page.) After spending a proper time at the Falls, and in looking through the immense lumber manufactories thereon, you drive through St. Anthony, observing the neatness of the buildings, the thrift and energy of her business men, and the rapid growth of the city. Having gained from editors or land agents what information, you may wish respecting the place, you drive across that magnificent structure, the wire suspension bridge,—the first that ever spanned the noble Mississippi. Having reached the western bank, you are in Minneapolis, a town which, for beauty of location and rapidity of growth, is scarcely excelled by any other in the Territory. Next you drive to the Minneapolis Hotel, where yourself and your team will be well cared for. Dr. Keith the gentlemanly proprietor, will cheerfully give you any general information respecting the town and country. Here is the United States land office, besides the land agencies of Messrs. Snyder and McFarlane, and Hancock and Thomas, where those who are looking for land, or desire to enter into a speculation, will not fail to call.

From Minneapolis you pass in a westerly direction nearly six miles to lakes Harriet and Calhoun, two beautiful, sparkling gems, encircled by a thin belt of thrifty young oaks. These lakes are each about three miles in length and two in width. The water is clear as crystal, and having a fine, pebbly beach. These lakes are filled with an abundance of fish.

Six miles farther and you are at Minnehaha Falls, probably the most romantic and beautiful cascade in the Union. The stream falls forty-five feet perpendicularly into a magnificent basin below. As the rock projects several feet, parties can travel entirely around, under the Falls.

One mile farther is Fort Snelling, the largest and most eligibly situated military post in the Territory. Here you are ferried across the Mississippi, and proceed to within two miles of St. Paul, where you find Fountain Cave. This is truly a curiosity. The cave appears to have been worn from the sand rock, in which it exists, by the pure crystal stream passing through it. At the entrance this cave is about fifteen feet in diameter, the opening decreasing in size as you proceed. The writer penetrated the cave several rods, and found the pure, soft, white sandstone to extend throughout its entire length. About three hundred feet from the mouth is a cascade, some six feet in height, beyond which the passage becomes contracted.

Two miles farther, and you are again at St. Paul, in time for tea, having visited St. Anthony City, St. Anthony, the Falls, the suspension bridge, Hennepin Island, Minneapolis, Lake Harriet, Lake Calhoun, Minnehaha Falls, Fort Snelling, Fountain Cave, and St. Paul, all in one day! Nowhere else on this continent can so much of interest and beauty be seen in so short a time.

Those who have time to tarry longer at the Falls will find stages leaving each of the hotels for St. Anthony, twice a day—at 7 o'clock A. M., and 2 P. M. A daily line of stages also runs up the beautiful valley of the Minnesota River to South Bend; another line to Stillwater, and daily or tri-weekly lines to the principal points of interest and importance.

CHAPTER V.

THE MINNESOTA (FORMERLY ST. PETERS) VALLEY.

By treaties made in 1851, with the Dakotah Indians, the United States Government obtained a title to the territory "lying between the Mississippi River on the east and the Big Sioux on the west, extending through four parallels of latitude and five degrees of longitude, and covering a superficial area of forty-five thousand square miles."

In the heart of this purchase, through rich alluvial lands, through savannas of luxuriant grass, through dense forests and through flowery prairies, the Minnesota River winds its course for hundreds of miles. Less than five years have elapsed since the red man held undisputed sway in this valley. Then he was the sole occupant, and could truly exclaim,

> "I am monarch of all I survey,
> My right there is none to dispute;"

and as, in his freedom, he roamed over the vast prairies and hunted through the deep shady forests, or lightly skipped the waters of the Minnetouka, he fearlessly and realizingly exclaimed,

> "I am lord of the fowl and the brute."

Five years have elapsed, and the traveller now finds the varied landscape of this beautiful valley dotted here and there with a residence or a farm-house, or, perchance, a thrifty yearling town, with its hundred buildings — stores, school-house, and church — the centre for a well-settled and thoroughly-tilled agricultural district; while, at proper distances along the valley, are erected grist and saw-mills, supplied from the large fields' fruitful yield, or with timber from the Bois Franc, or Great Woods, or from the numerous groves that beskirt the shores of this river and the lakes adjacent; for, in the language of John G. Whittier, our American poet:

> "Behind the red squaw's birch canoe
> The steamer smokes and raves,
> And city lots are staked for sale
> Above old Indian graves.
>
> "I hear the tread of pioneers
> Of nations yet to be —
> The first low wash of waves, where soon
> Shall roll a human sea."

Fort Snelling. — After leaving St. Paul, by land, the first point of interest reached is Fort Snelling, situated on the west side of the Mississippi River, at the junction of the Minnesota with the Mississippi, six miles above St. Paul. "The site is one of the most beautiful and picturesque imaginable, occupying the front or verge of the extensive plateau, at the angle formed by the confluence of the Minnesota with the Mississippi. The plateau or table-land, upon which the post is situated, rises abruptly from the banks of these streams to an elevation of one hundred feet, when it merges into a level plain, stretching in the rear as far as the eye can reach, and unbroken, except by the indentation of streams and limpid lakes, which here and there lay embosomed upon its surface." This site was purchased by Lieutenant Pike in 1805. In 1819 the fort buildings were erected, and the fort established, under the supervision of Colonel Snelling, from whom it derives its name. This fort, being no longer needed for the purposes for which it was originally erected, is now used principally as a rendezvous for soldiers, and as a storehouse where supplies are held for points farther interior.

From this point, up the Minnesota valley, the road passes over a beautiful prairie, skirted in the distance, on the north by woods along Minnetouka or Little Falls Creek, and on the south by the beautiful, well-timbered valley of the Minnesota. Sixteen miles from St. Paul, Oak Grove, a fine body of woodland, is reached. One mile farther, and you reach Mr. Gibson's farmhouse, where you will find an excellent dinner, — which, by the way, you may not be sure of at every stopping-place. Thence to Shakopee the road is over a prairie, skirted with oak openings or groves along the valley.

CHAPTER VI.

TOWNS AND VILLAGES IN THE MINNESOTA VALLEY.

SHAKOPEE is the county-seat of Scott county, and is twenty-five miles southwest of St. Paul by land and thirty by water; is beautifully situated on an elevated plateau, gradually sloping back from the Minnesota River for two miles to a forest of tall heavy trees. The town plat embraces three hundred and twenty acres, which is liberally laid off into large lots and wide, roomy streets. This place has many natural advantages, among which may be enumerated, a good landing and large levee, on a river which is navigable to this point all seasons of the year; an abundance of timber-land in adjacent groves, with saw-mills to manufacture lumber; excellent clay for brick, and several lime-kilns, which supply, not only the wants of this place, but those of the towns above.

A gentleman who has worked for a long number of years in the Galena lead mines, stated to me that he found indications of lead in the vicinity of Shakopee. So certain is he of the existence of lead at a particular point, that he is endeavoring to negotiate a lease of the land, in order to commence mining.

Add to these the elevated, healthy site for residences, with clear cold water bubbling up from the earth in numerous springs; and you have advantages which a prince might envy.

Shakopee stands on the site of an Indian village, occupied, till within the past three years, by the band of Shakopee, or Little Six, a noted chief among the Sioux. It now contains about 800 inhabitants, principally from the East. Here are two churches, an ably-conducted newspaper, good schools, and many of the refinements of larger and older towns. The Wasson receives and deserves an extensive patronage. A new three-story brick hotel is being erected, also several warehouses and stores, brick, stone, and frame. This town has had an unprecedented growth, and is still improving rapidly and substantially. In the township in which Shakopee is situated are nine lakes, varying from half a mile to two miles in width. In Scott county are five other towns: Belle Plaine, Louisville, Jordan, Mount Pleasant, and Bellefontaine.

Mount Pleasant is situated on Long Lake, about six miles from Shakopee, and is represented as being an eligible site for a town. On the outlet of this lake is a saw and grist-mill, doing well. This town has been but recently laid out, and offers a chance for beginners.

Bellefontaine is situated on the banks of Spring

Lake, eight miles from Shakopee. This lake contains myriads of fish of the finest quality; the adjoining woods abound in wild game of various kinds, while from its banks gush forth, in never-failing springs, an abundance of pure cold water. The proprietors offer great inducements to mill-wrights and mechanics.

Jordan City, eleven miles above Shakopee, and one mile from the river, is the first town reached on the road leading to Mankato. Here are one grist and two saw-mills, hotel, plough factory, and 100 inhabitants; merchants and mechanics are wanted.

Belle Plaine is well named. It is situated upon one of the most beautiful prairies in the valley, about midway between St. Paul and South Bend. It is surrounded by timber lands of the best quality, has a good landing for steamboats, is a pleasant and healthy locality for a home, and a good opening for business men. Hon. A. G. Chatfield, associate judge, resides here, and is one of the proprietors. The town is new, though it contains two hotels, a saw-mill, etc., and is being settled by persons of intelligence and energy.

Yorkville, on the opposite bank, a short distance above Shakopee, is settled principally by Germans. They projected this town as the river point for Lake Minnetouka, which is seven miles distant; but this cannot be accomplished until a road is made across an almost impassable intervening swamp.

Chaska, three miles above, has a good location, and is in a prosperous condition. Here Mr. Oliver Farribault formerly had an extensive trading establishment. The place was then known as "Little Prairie," and was settled principally by Canadians, most of whom left with him.

Carver, three miles above Chaska, is at the mouth of Carver's Creek. "The rapid increase of settlements in the vicinity, and the energy with which the proprietors are pushing their improvements, give promise of a quick and healthy growth."

Louisville is two miles below the rapids, and is the centre for numerous settlements, made last year and still making; but the location forbids of a very extensive settlement.

San Francisco, the county-seat of the county of Carver, is on the north side of the river, a short distance above the rapids. Its location is pleasant and advantageous, and during seasons of high water it commands the business at the rapids.

Between Shakopee and Belle Plaine, the road passes over some very poor soil. Sand Prairie, just above Jordan, is three miles in length and one to one and three-quarters in width, bounded on the south by the Great Woods, and on the north by a marsh or flat a mile or more in width, reaching to the river, and extending some distance along the valley.

Henderson, the county-seat of Sibley county, is a centrally located town, of much thrift and energy. "The location is altogether too low, and in the midst of a dense forest." These objections have been urged. Embankments are being made, which will protect the town from high water; and the giant oaks are fast giving way to residences and business blocks. Henderson is the landing for a large and rapidly settling portion of country. The roads from the river westward are tolerable; those from above or below, along the river, almost intolerable. J. R. Brown, Esq., publishes here one of the best country-town papers in the Territory, and, if Henderson does not become a large and populous city, it will not be *his* fault, nor will it be because the wants of a large and populous country do not demand a commercial point thereabouts, but for the reasons above mentioned. Roads from Fort Ridgely, from Red Wing, from St. Paul, and from Sauk Rapids, centre at this point. This place contains two hotels, four stores, one steam saw-mill, and about 300 inhabitants.

Clarksville, a new town, just laid out on the opposite side of the river, is situated on a more elevated site, and promises to improve rapidly. The ferry at this point is doing a good business.

Le Sueur, the county-seat of Le Sueur county, is five miles above Henderson and sixty from St. Paul. The town, though of less than a year's growth, contains two saw-mills, three hotels, three stores, and dwellings in proportion. Cabinet-makers, carpenters, and blacksmiths are wanted. Actual settlers can hear of good claims of timber near the river, by applying to J. S. Perry, tailor, at Le Sueur. The town is situated on a sloping prairie, gradually rising from the river, not very unlike the site of Peoria, Ill. This prairie is nine miles in length and four in width, surrounded by a heavy forest of timber. Le Sueur county contains a population of upwards of 2500, and is rapidly filling up. In this county also are Lexington, situated on the west side of Cedar Lake, ten miles east; Scotch Lake, twelve miles southeast, where a large steam saw-mill and other improvements are being erected; Waterville, thirty miles southeast, a snug little village, having a post-office and water-mills. Lake Elysian, twenty-five miles southeast, is situated on a fine lake of the same name, and is rapidly building up; Ottowa, on the Minnesota River, six miles above Le Sueur, has a fine saw-mill, and will be a nucleus for a large, well-settled neighborhood. After a ride of seven miles, you reach Traverse de Sioux (the crossing of the Sioux), one of the oldest settlements in the Territory, and the county-seat of Nicollet county. In 1823, the Columbia Fur Company established a post here, and changed the mode of transporting supplies, and exchanges — abandoning the Mackinaw boats and introducing the use of carts instead, which are still employed by the Red River traders of the North. "This being the lowest point on the Minnesota River that could be reached without passing through timber, the place in a short time became a depot for the entire trade of the upper Sioux, and a general rendezvous for Indians near and remote." The population of Traverse de Sioux is about 600. Mills and mechanics are much needed, and would give a new impetus to this naturally important point.

St. Peter's is a newly laid out town, seventy-two miles above St. Paul, forty-three above Shakopee, and about twelve below South Bend. The site of this town is beautifully and advantageously located. It contains saw and grist-mills, warehouses and stores, four hotels (a two-story one of stone), and a well-conducted newspaper, published by the company. Opposite the town lies Spring Lake and several chalybeate springs. St. Peter contains about 400 inhabitants, and is improving rapidly. The prairie, on which this town and Traverse are located, is one of the handsomest in the valley.

Kasota, three miles above St. Peter, is a new place, properly situated for a good manufacturing town. The outlet from Lake Washington has here a fall of twenty-two feet, which is as yet but partially improved. A small steamboat and a flat boat are being built here. Another mill is building on this outlet, six miles from Kasota.

CHAPTER VII.

THE GREAT SOUTH BEND AND THE BLUE EARTH COUNTRY.

MANKATO is situated eighty miles above St. Paul, and four miles below the most southerly point of the "great south bend of the St. Peter's (now Minnesota) River." It contains some sixty buildings, three stores, hotel, etc. A large steam-mill was in course of erection in July. There has been a dispute between two of the proprietors, about the town plat, and good titles could not be obtained. This fact has retarded the growth of the place, and done much to increase the sale of lots in Mankato city, a town adjoining on the river, below, belonging to a St. Paul land agent. Owing to the scarcity of lumber, few buildings are being erected this season. When the title to lots shall have been settled, and this steam-mill completed, the citizens anticipate a better state of things. This is the county-seat of Blue Earth county; some idea of the growth of which may be gained from the facts that in 1853 the total amount of personal property subject to taxation was less than $3000, while in 1855 it amounted to $40,000, and this year, 1856, to $142,277.50! Information of this town or county may be learned from Robert Wardlaw, Esq., merchant at Mankato.

Mankato is the river point for the Winnebago Indian Agency, twelve miles distant. (See chapter on " Indian tribes in Minnesota.")

South Bend is a town recently laid out, four miles above Mankato, on the extreme south bend of the Minnesota River. The Blue Earth River, one mile below, is bridged near its mouth with a trestle bridge, which cost $10,000, and which is being erected by government, on the United States mail road leading from St. Paul to Sioux City, Iowa, on the Missouri River. This road leaves the river at South Bend, and strikes southwest to Sioux City. The landing on the river is excellent, having a natural and easy grade into the town. The high, level plateau, upon which the town is located, is sufficiently extensive for the depot grounds of the various railroads in contemplation, or as the site of the great commercial emporium which the geographical situation of the country and the wants of the people demand at this point.

The south bend of the Minnesota has long been looked upon as possessing local advantages which promise, at no distant day, to insure the building up of a large commercial city, which shall be the centre of this unequalled agricultural district, and the terminus of at least two important railroads from Iowa: one from Clinton, *via* Cedar Rapids, or from Dubuque; the other from Fort Dodge and the capital of the State, tapping her rich beds of coal and gypsum.

Whether Mankato or South Bend shall be *the city* depends somewhat upon the energy of the proprietors and citizens of each, but principally upon the feasibility of routes for railroads to the river, at either point.

THE BLUE EARTH COUNTRY.—One of the most fertile and most beautiful portions of the Territory lies between South Bend and the Iowa line. Of this region, M. Nicollet, in his report of the "Hydrographic Basin of the Upper Mississippi," says: "I shall now proceed to give a short account of some of the regions of country adjoining the *Coteau des Prairies.* Among these, that which appeared to me most favorable is the one watered by the 'Bold Mankato' or Blue Earth River, and to which I have given the name of 'Undine Region.'

"The great number of navigable tributaries of the Blue Earth, spreading themselves out in the shape of a fan; the group of lakes, surrounded by well-wooded hills; some wide-spreading prairies with a fertile soil; others apparently less favored, but open to improvement—the whole of them together bestow upon this region a most picturesque appearance."

Speaking of this point on the river, and of the country surrounding, J. Wesley Bond says:

"Here it is, upon the glittering banks of two silvery streams of spacious capacity, with fertile prairies, opening to the warm, sunny south, sweeping off for miles and miles till the closing vista is bounded by fringes of forests, while, in the rear, close to the banks of the river, stands heavy timber, ready for the builder's hands, to be converted into domiciles of comfort or elegance."

On the Wattonwon and other tributaries of the Blue Earth are numerous mill privileges, unimproved, with an abundance of water power and timber land, and centrally located for grist-mills. Some of these sites were subject to pre-emption in July last, when I travelled through this country.

In October, 1854, the first claims were made between the Wattonwon and Blue Earth; in July, 1856, every one hundred and sixty acre tract was "claimed" and settled. One claim was shown me which was sold the week before for $2000. As to the fertility of the soil, I need only say, I saw on these streams as fine crops, taking all kinds of grain into account, as there are in the Territory. A piece of prairie, broken last fall, and sown with wheat, harrowed in this spring, yields a fraction less than fifty bushels to the acre! How will that do for a *sod crop?*

CHAPTER VIII

THE MINNESOTA ABOVE SOUTH BEND.

THE Minnesota River is navigable a portion of every year, as high up as Yellow Medicine, four hundred and fifty miles. The distances from St. Paul to the numerous towns on this river may be seen by reference to the table of distances on another page.

Eureka, at the outlet of Swan Lake, twenty-five miles above South Bend, has a beautiful location, and is surrounded by a very fertile district of country.

My friend, Mr. Phillips, of the Shakopee Independent, having made a trip to the Upper Sioux Agency since I left the Territory, I give his account, which I am ready to vouch as correct in all particulars. He says: "The numerous well-improved farms which line the road from Shakopee to Belle Plain, bear every evidence of prosperity and industry. The vast fields of waving grain show that the farmers have made ample preparations for an extensive harvest, and their expectations are about to be realized; and who is more worthy to receive that reward than the tiller of the soil?

"Belle Plain, on the Minnesota River, although an old familiar point, has been but recently located as a town site, under the auspices of Hon. A. G. Chatfield and others, and bears evident signs of improvement and go-aheaditiveness. It is beautifully located, and, with the advantages with which it is surrounded to recommend it to favorable notice, must become the nucleus of a large and thriving settlement.

"Next morning's sunrise finds us dashing over the prairies; and one who has not felt the delightful sensation that is experienced from a gallop at this hour can form but an imperfect idea of its effect upon the system. The spirits rise perceptibly, the heart expands, and a new, strange feeling pervades the whole frame. One who will pursue this mode of exercise can laugh disease to scorn.

"We pass through the 'Big Woods,' and our road is dotted numerously with fine, well-improved farms.

"The road from Henderson to Fort Ridgely lies through an almost unbroken prairie, and the land, with very few exceptions, remains unclaimed. Situated as it is, possessing but few attractions to recommend it to favorable notice, it must remain so for a long time to come. The land is excellent, but wood and water, those two great *desideratums* to settlers, cannot be procured.

"Fort Ridgely is situated on the Minnesota River, about two hundred miles from its mouth, on the Sioux reservation. The fort consists of two large stone houses, two stories in height, and about three hundred feet in length. There is nothing very striking or warlike in its appearance, but a quiet, comfortable outpost. There are at present eight companies quartered at this point, four of which are awaiting marching orders for Fort Pierre, on the Missouri River. About seventy military tents dot the prairie in the neighborhood of the fort, and, with that display and bustle incidental to military life, present a novel and interesting sight.

"Heartily tired of horse locomotion, we reached the lower Sioux Agency on Saturday evening, a distance of ninety miles from Shakopee City, on the Minnesota River. There is at this point several Indian trading posts, which, by order of the Government, are kept in operation the entire year. It is also the place of residence of the Indian farmer and physician; about ten white people include the whole population. A terrific hail-storm visited this place a few days before our arrival, which destroyed about two hundred acres of corn, planted by the Sioux; thus cutting off, in a great measure, their means of support. The inhabitants averred that hail fell as large as eggs; and, although several days had elapsed since the storm, we saw indentations in the earth which led us to believe that the report was correct.

"While at the Agency, we were the guest of the resident physician, Dr. Daniels, to whom we are indebted for many kind attentions. The ladies composing the household were refined and courteous, and we shall long remember with pleasure our Sabbath at the Agency.

"We noticed, on the route from the Agency to Red Wood, a large number of neat-looking log houses, and evident signs of agricultural improvement, which we learnt are the work of 'Shakopee's' and 'Little Crow's' band. The Indian is slowly beginning to realize the fact, that it is far better to turn his attention to the cultivation of the earth than to rely upon the uncertainties of the chase for a subsistence; and, although it is hard for them to overcome their prejudices, and their natural antipathy of imitation of the whites, there is a decided progressive spirit perceptible, which argues well for a better state of things than have heretofore existed among them.

"Yellow Medicine, or Upper Sioux Agency, is situated in a wild, romantic spot, in a valley through which a rivulet dashes along a narrow, rocky defile, associated with many a wild tale and stirring legend of Indian life, which needs but the inspiration of the scene, and the pen of the novelist, to weave into story. We fancied it was such a spot as this, and such scenes as this, that inspired the pen of Campbell, that gave to the world his poem of 'Gertrude of Wyoming.'

"A convocation of the principal chiefs of the bands in attendance was held at the office of the agent, R. G. Murphy, the morning after our arrival.

They represented themselves as being in an extreme destitute condition; but their demands for provisions and pay met with a firm and decided refusal from the agent, who informed them that none would be issued until the party who were engaged in the Chippewa murders were given up for punishment. Fourteen of these Indians, belonging to various bands of the Sioux, are now in custody at Fort Ridgely, and the remaining offenders, two in number, will probably be delivered up by the tribe, after which the payment will immediately take place. The prompt action of the superintendent and agent in regard to this matter will have a good effect in restraining the Sioux from hereafter waging war against the Chippewas.

"We looked in vain for that proud, haughty bearing that we had been led to suppose existed among them in their councils. Their spirits seem to be crushed, and there is a tame submissiveness manifest, which but ill accords with the wild, untamable spirit with which writers have invested them. Once only, when the agent severely reprimanded them for their warlike disposition, one old chieftain arose, and something like 'the pride of former days' seemed to animate him as he replied haughtily, and with emphatic gestures, that 'he had fought his enemies from his boyhood, and he had killed a large number of them, and he intended to kill a great many more before he died.' Observing the agent gazing on his bared and swarthy body, he exclaimed bitterly, 'You look at me as if you think I was poor: I am. You would be, too, if you had not tasted food for three days, as I have not.'

"A chief from the Sissitons represented to the agent, that it was impossible for his band to attend the payment, unless provisions were forwarded to aid them on their journey, as their women and children were weak and famishing for want of food, and unable to endure the hardships of the travel. The agent, with commendable promptness, immediately dispatched the necessary articles to meet them on their route.

"Heartily sick and tired of the misery and degradation that we saw existing among them, we gladly, next morning, took our way homeward, without witnessing the payment, which was to occur about the 1st of August."

English Travellers' Opinions of this Valley. — I can close my description of the valley of the Minnesota in no better words than those furnished in the reports of an English traveller, of great renown, named Carver, who visited this valley in 1766. He speaks of the Minnesota as flowing "through a most delightful country, abounding with all the necessaries of life, that grow spontaneously. Wild rice grows here in great abundance; and every part is filled with trees, bending under their loads of fruit, such as plums, grapes, and apples. The meadows are covered with hops, and many sorts of vegetables, while the ground is stored with useful roots—with angelica, spikenard, and ground-nuts as large as hens' eggs." He also speaks of a "milk-white clay" abounding near the south bend, on the Blue Earth, "out of which chinaware might be made, equal in goodness to the Asiatic;" and also of "a blue clay, which serves the Indians for paint."

Seventy years later, in 1835, G. W. Featherstonhaugh, F. R. S., a distinguished geologist, ascended the Minnesota, on an exploring tour, and describes the country about the mouth of the Blue Earth as "extremely beautiful; the prairie occasionally coming down to the waters' edge, while, at other times, bold bluffs arise, with well-wooded slopes, interspersed with graceful clumps of trees." Again, he speaks of the "charming slopes, with pretty dells intersecting them, studded with trees as gracefully as if they had been planted with the most refined taste, backed by thousands of well-formed trees, — thousands of acres of the most fertile land, with the river in front, and a world of prairie in the rear."

CHAPTER IX.

THE FALLS OF ST. ANTHONY.

MINNEAPOLIS, county-seat of Hennepin county, and St. Anthony (now in the same county), are situated upon the Mississippi River, fifteen miles above St. Paul by the river, and nine miles by land. At this point are the Falls of St. Anthony, the first impassable obstruction to the navigation of the Mississippi above the Gulf of Mexico. Between these cities, but nearer the eastern shore, are three islands which divide the river, the principal portion of the water passing on the Minneapolis or western side of the islands. Here the river falls seventeen feet perpendicularly, over a limestone rock. These falls have been a point of attraction for years past, and will ever continue to be. The number of visitors will annually increase, just in proportion as the beauty and magnificence of the scenery on the upper Mississippi, and the grandeur of these cataracts, "the crowning glory of the northwest," are made known to the admirers of nature's works in the East and the sunny South. As early as 1680, Louis Hennepin, a French Recollet Friar, a missionary and North American explorer, "gave to the foaming waters of St. Anthony's Falls their baptismal name, in honor of his patron saint."

By the Dahcotah or Sioux Indians, these falls are called Minnehaha (laughing water), and also Minne-o-wah (falling water). By the Ojibways they are called Kaboh-Bikah (the broken rocks). The former name, Minnehaha, is now only applied to the beautiful little falls between Minneapolis and Fort Snelling.

The Falls of St. Anthony are at present seven miles from the mouth of the Minnesota River. "It is, however," says Owen, United States geologist, "more than probable that they once occupied a position at or near Fort Snelling." Of course, little evidence can be gathered of the rate of wearing, from actual observation of the inhabitants recently settled there; but, judging from the condition of the strata themselves, there must have been a retrocession. The cement, which holds together the particles of the St. Peter's sandstone, is so slight, that it is with difficulty a solid specimen can be obtained. Yet this rock, with a covering of only fifteen or twenty feet of schistose limestone, to protect it from the swift current of the Mississippi, forms the base of the falls. The confused heaps of disjointed masses of limestone, piled together below the falls, indicate the undermining action in progress. The inclined position, too, of the ledges of limestone there, for several hundred yards above the chute, contrary to the local dip, has mostly been produced by the water which sweeps over them, entering the extensive rents which run across the strata at this place, gradually washing out the particles of sand upon which these ledges repose; thus allowing them gradually to sink, and causing huge blocks to become, from time to time, detached and precipitated into the rapids beneath. In this way, the fall will, probably, after a lapse of time, be converted into a rapid. For, in proportion as the fall shall recede, the sandstone, by reason of its dip, will diminish in thickness in the gorge, and at length disappear beneath the river bed. From observations of the dip at the falls, this latter contingency will occur when the fall has been worn back some six or seven miles from its present position.

The falls in the main channel are several rods above those in the eastern, the great volume of water having worn away the soft, crumbling rock much faster. The falls are at present seven miles from the mouth of the Minnesota, at Fort Snelling. An early voyager represents the falls as having been sixty feet in height; but I have been able to find no point between Fort Snelling and the present fall, where the geological formation warrants this conclusion: they are now but seventeen feet in height. However, Professor Owen mentions the discovery of a bed of drift, eleven feet in thickness, overlaying the limestone at the falls, extending half a mile below and east of the gorge. This formation is such as to warrant the conclusion that a lake once existed here, and that its outlet was a fall, much higher than the present, at or near Fort Snelling.

The last dislodgment of rock in the bed of the falls, occurred on the 5th of July last, when a large mass, fifteen feet wide and a hundred feet long, gave way, removing the fall up the stream, on the Minneapolis side, fourteen feet.

Minnehaha Falls, a point of considerable note, and now becoming a place of resort, should not pass unnoticed. A Minnesota editor thus speaks of them:

"This name, Minne-ha-ha, signifying laughing water, is given by the Dacotah Indians to a beautiful waterfall between Fort Snelling and St. Anthony's Falls. It is a favorite custom with the citizens of St. Paul, and of strangers visiting that locality, to drive to Fort Snelling, and from thence to St. Anthony's Falls, taking Minne-ha-ha in their way, and to return by a shorter and more direct route.

"Fort Snelling is situated upon a bluff, at the point where the Minnesota River empties into the Mississippi, about seven miles distant from St. Paul. Having crossed the river in a boat, and wound around the base of the bluff, you ascend to the plateau, on which stands the fort. Here you see stretching out before you an extensive prairie, with some rolling ground lying on the right hand, toward the upper Mississippi. In the course of a pleasant drive across the prairie, the excursionist comes suddenly upon a stream, about three rods wide, which glides quietly but rather swiftly along, the banks of which are skirted by a few bushes and small trees.

"The stranger would proceed on his route, and cross the stream, without suspecting the proximity of the falls of Minne-ha-ha; but those acquainted with the locality seek a point below the crossing, tie up their teams to one of the small trees, and, after a few rods into the sparse timber, find themselves upon the banks of a deep ravine, into which the miniature river enters by a downright plunge of fifty feet, and then runs away in a quiet manner, as if stunned by the fall from the prairies above. Clambering down the bank by the aid of projecting roots and shrubs, you approach the fall of the Laughing Water, which whitens into foam as it descends, and drives up a cloud of spray from the pool below. The water is poured over a shelf of rock in semi-circular form, as regularly shaped as if fashioned by a Yankee mechanic, and under this shelf visitors pass behind the fall around to the opposite side, dry-shod. A neater waterfall than this could not be whittled out with the jack-knife; and this is the Minne-ha-ha—Laughing Water—

after which Mr. Longfellow has named the interesting squaw described in his story of Hiawatha."

By the table of contents, find "The Sight-seer's Diurnal Drive," in another chapter, where full directions for visiting Minne-ha-ha are given.

CHAPTER X.

ST. ANTHONY AND MINNEAPOLIS.—THEIR ADVANTAGEOUS POSITION, BUSINESS STATISTICS, ETC.

FROM the year 1849 may be dated the commencement of St. Anthony, though one cabin had stood here for twelve years previous. The present population of the place is about 3500. The lumbering business is at present the great manufacturing interest of St. Anthony. Eight saws are in constant operation, capable of manufacturing twelve million feet of lumber per annum; in addition to which, another gang of saws have recently been put in operation, which will probably cut five million feet per annum. This mill is located on the dam leading from the main shore to Hennepin Island. To this dam are sixteen apertures for mills, nine of which are now occupied. It is expected that more mills will be erected next season, and all the apertures will be filled at as early a day as possible. Ten million feet of logs can be packed in the dam. The proprietors will enlarge the dam another season, by extending it out into the river from the upper end of Hennepin Island, so as to increase the water power, and some five million feet more of logs.

In addition to the above is a shingle and lath machine, which saws thirteen thousand shingles and twenty thousand laths per day.

The admirable situation of St. Anthony for manufacturing purposes is the first idea that strikes the mind, as one surveys its location. Situated on the great "Father of Waters," whose supply never fails; the banks (above the cataract) almost level with the water; a descent of some sixty feet within a mile; the channel conveniently divided by islands, easy of access, and affording unequalled facilities for the economical use of water power, both banks being capable of being sluiced for a mill, and the water used to an unlimited extent; abundance of stone at hand suitable for the erection of manufacturing edifices—all these form a combination of advantages seldom found in one locality. Add to this that it is at the head of navigation on the Mississippi, surrounded by an agricultural district which is excelled by none in the Union, which produces in rich luxuriance all the cereals, is admirably adapted to fruit, and unsurpassed for grazing, and you have all the elements to constitute a great manufacturing metropolis. The location of St. Anthony is also exceedingly favorable for controlling a large amount of country trade. The county of Hennepin, and all the north part of Ramsey and Benton counties, are natural auxiliaries and tributaries of this place. The capital invested in business in St. Anthony is as follows: banking, $150,000; merchandizing, $280,000; manufacturing, $125,000; livery, $15,000; saloons, $100,000.

Minneapolis is beautifully situated on the west bank of the Mississippi, directly opposite to the City of St. Anthony. The bank of the river above the falls is low, rising in uneven bluffs from five to twenty-five feet, gradually ascending for about a hundred rods back from the stream.

The name is an Indian and Greek compound, "Minneha," being the Sioux term for water, and "polis," the Greek word for city—"City of Water." Colonel J. H. Stevens was the first settler of Minneapolis, and erected his dwelling in the winter of 1849–50. Speaking of his early residence and neighbors, the Colonel says: "We have often retired at night and opened our eyes in the morning upon the wigwams of either the Sioux, Chippewa, or Winnebago, which had gone up while we slept."

Minneapolis is located on what was formerly known as the "Military Reserve of Fort Snelling," a reservation of nine miles square, around the fort, for the purposes of forage; and it was not until the 5th of March, 1855, that Congress passed an act granting the right of pre-emption to settlers, so that the really permanent growth of Minneapolis has all taken place since that period. The present population is about 2000. Amount of capital employed: in merchandizing, $120,000; in manufacturing, $60,000; in livery, $10,000.

The suspension bridge between St. Anthony and Minneapolis is worthy of notice. As a work of beauty and art, it can hardly be surpassed, while at the same time it has the appearance of great durability and solidity; its massive cables being firmly anchored on either side in the solid rock. The work was undertaken in the spring of 1854, and completed about 1st July, 1855. The company have expended something over $50,000 on this work, and certainly have occasion to be proud of their labors, for it is the first suspension bridge ever built in a Territory, and the first to span the " Fathers of Waters."

Perhaps nothing more forcibly illustrates the rapid growth of the population around the falls than the increase of ferriage and tolls at the bridge. In 1851, Franklin Steele established a ferry there, and realized, during the summer, $300; in 1852, $1,100; in 1853, $2,700; in 1854, $6,000; and in 1855, $12,000. It is estimated that the receipts of the present year will not be less than $25,000.

Those desiring information about this place, or of the surrounding country, cannot do better than apply to Messrs. Snyder & McFarlane, land agents, who are supplied with maps and other important data, which, through their gentlemanly politeness, are tendered to those who may visit this region in quest of information.*

Colonel Stevens, the first settler, who has watched the rise and progress of this place, thus speaks of the future: "We now look for a more rapid growth for Minneapolis than has characterized any other town in the Territory. Everything indicates that it must, at some day not far distant, become one of the most important towns in the Territory. Its water privileges and manufacturing advantages are unequalled. It is surrounded by a magnificent farming country, the very garden of Minnesota. It has been settled by a population, which, for energy, education, enterprise, and industry, has nowhere a superior.

"Within another five years, and when two or three more bridges shall have spanned the Mississippi, we look to see Minneapolis and St. Anthony united under one corporation, and constituting one great city, which will know no superior northwest of Chicago, in point of population, enterprise, and wealth."

This point is a gem of a place — the centre set of nature's brilliants, around which she has placed Lakes Calhoun, Harriet, Clear Lake, Minnetouka, and that bright particular gem, Minne-ha-ha!

* The author would here tender his thanks to Dr. G. H. Keith, of the Minneapolis House, and to W. A. Hotchkiss, Esq., editor of the N. W. Democrat, for items of importance, and special favors tendered him, during his sojourn with them.

CHAPTER XI.

THE RIVER MISSISSIPPI ABOVE THE FALLS.

THE description of country extending north from Clinton, Iowa, is found again above the Falls of St. Anthony. There is no charm — the banks are low, the large rolling prairies, clothed with grass and flowers, extending to the water's edge, interspersed here and there with small groves, or oak openings. Along the west bank, for some distance, a dense forest extends as far as the eye can reach, principally of maple, elm, cottonwood, oak, and hackberry; and the islands that occur here and there in the channel are covered with a heavy undergrowth, or with trees as above named. The eminences or high points that occur along in the distance are crowned with a heavy growth of deep green pine trees.

The Mississippi is navigable for some hundreds of miles above the falls, and boats run regularly between St. Anthony and Sauk Rapids. Towns and villages are springing up, and growing into importance, each the centre of a thickly-settled agricultural district.

Manomin, a new town, seven miles above St.

Anthony, contains several dwellings, stores, hotel, etc., and an excellent saw-mill.

Anoka is beautifully situated, at the mouth of St. Francis or Rum River, eighteen miles above the falls. A dam, saw and grist-mill, have been erected here, costing $30,000; and numerous other manufactories are under contract. With the very extensive water-power, an abundance of pine timber, and surrounded by a fertile farming country, this place is worthy the attention of those wishing to locate.

At Elk River there will be a flourishing town at no distant day. A good water-power has already been rendered available, and the soil is very generally being subdued by active and intelligent men, who have extended their operations for miles up the river.

The next town of importance is Monticello, situated about midway between St. Anthony's Falls and Sauk Rapids. The town site is laid out on a beautiful sloping prairie, possessing a good river landing. Besides the steam saw-mill, sash and door factory, etc., there are numerous other manufactories in course of erection. An island lying upon the west side, about one third of the way across, would render this point a feasible one for bridging, there being but one water pier necessary. Monticello is the county-seat of Wright county, and bids fair to become a large place. Nearly every claim (one hundred and sixty acres), for thirty miles west, is taken; and why should n't it be? The soil, for strength and richness, is scarcely excelled in the Territory, timber and prairie being about equally divided.

Humboldt is the name of a new town recently laid out by Joseph Brown, Esq., and is the county-seat of Sherburne county. The location of this town is delightful, being immediately upon the shore of Big Lake, a sheet of water seldom surpassed for beauty. The surrounding country is pleasant, and the soil is rich and adapted to a high grade of cultivation. A large and most beautiful prairie, two and a half miles wide, stretches out magnificently from the village of Humboldt to the Mississippi River, inclining gracefully the whole distance, whereby the inhabitants of the county-seat of Sherburne county enjoy a charming view of Monticello, which is located immediately on the opposite side of the river, and upon a prairie ascending gradually as it recedes westwardly for five miles, skirted by a magnificent forest.

Benton City, at the head of steamboat navigation, is a new and pleasantly situated town, one hundred miles above the falls by river, and seventy-four by land.

St. Cloud City is situated on the west side of the river, a short distance below the mouth of Sauk River, at the foot of the rapids, and of course at the head of steamboat navigation. It is the county-seat of Stearns county, the centre or crossing of a number of important roads, and its proprietors claim for this town, " the point of crossing Mississippi for the Great North Pacific Railroad to Puget Sound. For a description of the country in the rear of St. Cloud, through which the railroad must pass, you are referred to Gov. Stevens' official report to Government, of his survey and exploring expedition."

The Sauk rapids of the Mississippi, the first obstruction above St. Anthony's Falls, extend about a mile along the river, and will, with a comparatively small expenditure of capital, furnish a very extensive water-power. The town of Sauk Rapids is situated about a mile above St. Cloud, and directly opposite the rapids is the county-seat of Benton county, which contains a United States land office. The citizens of this place, upon the authority of Mr. Lander, contend that upon the fine hard granite rock of these rapids is the best point above St. Paul for the Pacific Railroad bridge. This town is well located, and will become one of importance.

Four miles above the rapids is Watab, an old Indian trading fort, which is not destined to be much larger than at present. Opposite Watab, on the west shore, is " Watab Prairie," a beautiful and fertile piece of land. Between Watab and Platte River the land is nearly all prairie, except along the banks of the Little Rock and Platte Rivers. Several claims have recently been made, and this extensive prairie will soon be well settled along either bank of the Mississippi.

Along the Platte River are some of the best cultivated farms in this section. What is known as "the old Depue farm" is one of the finest in Benton county, well fenced, well stocked, and with as large a barn as there is in the Territory. Seven years ago, Mr. Depue and wife squatted here, with nothing but a yoke of oxen, a wagon, and a few articles of household furniture. With persevering industry and economy, they have secured a farm, which, for neatness and extent, like the social and hospitable qualities of its owners, is spoken of by all travellers passing that way. Above this, from Coon Creek to Fort Ripley, extends an almost continuous tamarisk swamp, coming in some instances to the river, and in others receding several miles back. Where the swamp extends to the river, the road is almost impassable. Here are the first pine trees seen on the Mississippi. There are no heavy bodies of pine timber, however, until you have passed some distance above Crow Wing.

Three miles above Swan River is Little Falls, a beautiful place, with an extensive water power. It has a fine farming country all around it, with a good rich soil to work upon. A saw-mill was built here some four years ago. Its original proprietors were officers of the army and highly respectable civilians of the Territory.

Four miles above, ten miles from Fort Ripley, is

Belle Prairie; and well does it deserve the name. Mr. Ayer, formerly a missionary among the Indians, settled here some six years ago, and is now surrounded by several families. He first commenced the opening of a farm and the erection of buildings for a manual labor school for half-breeds and whites. A handsome framed school-house and comfortable dwellings have been built, and the school was opened some four years ago.

The south line of the Fort Ripley military reserve extends down to within about one mile of Mr. Ayers'. Six miles further, is the house and farm of S. B. Olmstead. Mr. O. has a fine farm, under good cultivation, with a large comfortable house and barns. He is the contractor to the fort for the supply of beef and hay, besides supplying the officers and men with other produce of his farm.

On the west side of the river is Fort Ripley, with quarters, barracks, etc., all built of wood, inclosed on three sides by the buildings, and on the fourth by the river, a quadrangular piece of ground, of about three acres, beautifully ornamented. The houses of the officers, built facing each other, forming two right angles from the river, are of a cottage style, with a wide piazza, and are altogether very comfortable and convenient. All the buildings are kept handsomely painted, the ground neat and clean, which makes the fort present, from the river, a very pleasant and comfortable appearance. Nor is this appearance deceitful to a visitor at the fort, or at the quarters of the officers.

Seven miles above the fort is Crow Wing, a place at one time of some importance in the Indian trade, but now nearly all its business has been drawn to the Indian Agency, seven miles west, on the Crow Wing River. Crow Wing is an old settlement, and was for a long time the head-quarters for the small outfits into the Indian country. Living here is one of the old pioneers of the northwest, Mr. Allen Morrison, a man who, through a long life, has seen and felt the trials and troubles of the frontier.

The Indian trader is truly the pioneer of civilization. With a small pack of goods on his back, he penetrates into the wilds and forests of an unknown Indian country, and sees with a quick eye the advantages and resources of it. This soon becomes known, and following in his trail come, "like the rushing of mighty waters," the hardy and adventurous white settlers, who, with eager longing for the home of the Indian, cry to Congress for its purchase. It is accomplished; and the land of the Indians, of no use to them except for its game, becomes the happy home of civilized white men. But what becomes of the trader? His occupation is gone; old age has come upon him, and he is perhaps living in some obscure place, in poverty and neglect. It is true, almost without exception, that the small traders — the men who have done the work, who have packed eighty pounds of goods upon their backs, weeks and months together, trading with and collecting furs from the Indians — after spending the best years of their life in this way, are as poor as when they commenced. This is in part owing to the wasteful habits, acquired by residence among the Indians, but more to a system of policy acted upon by the larger traders, who, like Aaron's rod, swallow up all the smaller ones.

Farther up the Mississippi River the white settlements become more unfrequent. By a treaty, concluded in February of last year, the Chippewas have ceded all their lands east of the river, with the exception of certain specified reservations. The new purchase is chiefly valuable for its pine lumber; and will be brought into market as soon as the government surveys are completed.

The name Mississippi is of Indian origin; *Sepe* or *Sepim*, in Algonquin, signifying river, or running water. By De Soto, the river was called St. Louis, and by Count Frontenac, Colbert, in honor of M. Colbert, French minister of marine at the time of the explorations of Joliet and Marquette. The Indian appellation, however, has universally obtained; although, as used by the earlier writers and explorers, the orthography of the term was unfixed.*

* For numerous items of history, etc., in this chapter, the author returns thanks to the editor of the St. Paul Democrat.

CHAPTER XII.

THE ST. CROIX RIVER AND SURROUNDING COUNTRY.—POINT DOUGLAS, AFTON, HUDSON, LAKELAND, ARCOLA, MARINE MILLS, TAYLOR'S FALLS, AMIDON, AND SUNRISE.

IN the St. Croix country were made some of the earliest settlements in Minnesota; and, as will be seen by reference to the chapter on the lumber business, this district is one of the most important in the Territory. The reader will visit, with me, the principal points on the St. Croix.

Point Douglas is situated in the angle formed by the Mississippi River and Lake St. Croix, and was surveyed and laid out as a town in 1840. The first house in the place was erected in 1839. It is now considerable of a town, but not improving very rapidly. Opposite this place, on the Wisconsin shore, is Point Prescott, an excellent natural site for a town, with good landing on the river, and good country around. Philander Prescott, Esq., the first white settler in the St. Croix valley, built and located on this spot in the year 1837. Afton, a new town, recently staked off, has a fine agricultural country around it, and, if no other town comes in its way, may grow to be a large village. On either shore, as we pass along, the lake is full of logs, either floating about at the mercy of every wind and wave, or else lying, like huge alligators in the sun, upon the shore. Our boat, the "Granite State," Captain Hurd, had some difficulty in landing at Hudson, as the wind upon the lake was strong, and had driven thousands of logs ashore.

Hudson (Wisconsin), is beautifully located on the east shore of St. Croix Lake, twenty-two miles above its confluence with the Mississippi. Population 1500. It is St. Croix county-seat, and the location of the United States land office for the Hudson (formerly Willow River) land district. The village has doubled its population within the last fifteen months, and bids fair to increase in the same ratio for many years to come. It is easily accessible by any of the steamboats running on the upper Mississippi. Choice farms can be obtained in the immediate neighborhood of the village at Government prices. Twelve miles back choice locations can be had from Government. A railroad company has been organized, which proposes to build a road from Hudson to Superior City, at the head of Lake Superior,—a distance, according to the surveys, of one hundred and thirty-three miles.*

* For further particulars, see the Hudson North Star, an excellent newspaper.

Lakeland, in Washington county, is one of the most beautiful village sites in the St. Croix valley. It is situated on a beautiful level plain, above high-water mark, on the west bank of Lake St. Croix, nearly opposite the village of Hudson. It has but recently been surveyed into village lots, and already contains a population of over 100. It is surrounded by a country unsurpassed for agricultural purposes, and rapidly filling up with an industrious farming community, mills and manufactories are springing up, and mechanics will consider themselves invited to call and examine Lakeland.

Stillwater, first settled in October, 1843, is now a bustling, thriving, and busy city of several hundred inhabitants. It is situated one mile below the mouth of St. Croix River, and at the head of low-water (for large steamers) navigation. Being considered as a central and important point, I will mention that Stillwater is twenty-five miles above the mouth of the lake, twenty-five miles below Taylor's Falls, twenty-five east of St. Anthony's Falls, one hundred and fifty southwest of the head of Lake Superior, one hundred and fifty southwest of Sauk Rapids, one hundred and seventy northeast of South Bend, fifty northwest of La Crosse, eighteen miles east by land and fifty by water from St. Paul. The St. Croix Union (a Stillwater paper) anticipates that this point will be on the route of the Madison and St. Paul, and the Dubuque, St. Paul, and Superior City Railroads, besides being the terminus of a road from Green Bay. The statistics of the lumber business of this section are given in another chapter.

Stillwater is the centre of one of the richest farming districts in the Territory. Many fine farms are already opened and cultivated, yielding a rich reward to those who till the soil, and this is the point from which the greater portion of the supplies for the extensive pine region on the St. Croix, and its numerous tributaries, are drawn by teams, or carried by boats; and we know of no business which pays better than that of farming. At present the home demand far exceeds the supply. Choice farms can be obtained in the immediate neighborhood of Stillwater at from $5 to $30 per acre, and some Government land can yet be bought, but it is fifteen or twenty miles distant. Land situated six miles west is advertised at $6 per acre. City property is rather higher, in proportion: twenty-eight and a half acres in the city limits recently sold at $150 an acre, and $200 was refused by the purchaser the same day.

Stillwater is the county-seat of Washington county. The court-house is a frame building of good size. The Catholic, Methodist, Episcopalian and Presbyterian denominations each have comfortable and substantial houses, and we believe each of them is supplied with preaching every Sabbath.

Few towns anywhere are better supplied with

good and wholesome springs than is Stillwater. Every few rods may be seen a pure spring gushing from the hill-side, and dashing onward over its gravelly bed. There is one spring here which we should judge would fill a barrel every minute; and no drought nor season seems to diminish it — so we are reliably informed.

For about a quarter of a mile along the lake where the city of Stillwater stands, the bluffs have retreated from the lake in the form of a semicircle. The ground along the lake is but a few feet above high-water mark; and, for the distance of two streets, it is slightly ascending, until the bluffs are reached, which are about one hundred feet in height, beyond which are beautiful oak openings, and excellent farming land.

"The pineries proper are from fifty to one hundred miles north of us. The delta south of Stillwater, lying between Lake St. Croix and the Mississippi River, is as rich and fertile as any body of land of like dimensions to be found anywhere in the Union; indeed, the whole of Washington county is good for farming purposes. There is just now one drawback; and that is, too much of it is owned by land-sharks and speculators. They know it to be valuable, and that it is continually rising in value, and they, therefore, hold on with a vice-like grasp; but it is gradually passing out of their hands, and the time is not very distant when the road between St. Paul and Stillwater will be lined on either side with large, productive, and magnificent farms." — *Union.*

From Point Douglas to Stillwater, rolling oak openings and level prairies characterize the valley of the St. Croix. Here are found some of the finest and oldest farms in the Territory, although in places there is a scarcity of wood and water. From Stillwater to Marine Mills the appearance of the valley continues much the same. Three miles from Stillwater is Boutwell's settlement, embracing some dozen farms, in a high state of cultivation. Situated in this portion of the valley is Cornelian Lake, a charming sheet of water, whose edges are paved with agates and with cornelians, colored in all the shades of red, from a bright vermillion to a brown. From Marine Mills to Taylor's Falls, the face of the country is changed. Here the prairies and oak openings disappear, and a belt of timber commences, eighteen miles long and six to ten wide. In this tract are scattered numerous lakes, the largest of which are Marine, Chisago, and Green. The lakes abound in fish, and the woods in deer and elk. Two settlements of Swedes are located in this section; one on the eastern and northern shore of Marine Lake, and the other between Chisago Lake and Taylor's Falls. The former embraces twenty-four families, the latter a hundred; both together including a population of some 700 persons, mostly engaged in agricultural pursuits.

Arcola, seven miles above Stillwater, is a town of probably 200 persons, with three mills, shops, stores, etc.

Marine Mills, six miles farther, contains a mill and numerous dwellings. The lumber and logging business of this place is estimated to be $40,000 annually. This settlement was commenced in 1838, by members of the Marine Lumber Company.

Taylor's Falls, twenty miles farther, has a population of 300. The first settlement on the Minnesota side of the St. Croix was made here in 1837, by members of the Northwestern Lumber Company. This is now the most important point above Stillwater, and the commercial centre for a large lumbering district. This is at the head of navigation even for small steamers.

Amidon, a town recently surveyed and laid out, is situated nine miles above Taylor's Falls.

Sunrise, seventeen miles above Taylor's Falls, on Sunrise River, is a small agricultural settlement, and contains two taverns. The land in the vicinity is good, and on Sunrise River are water powers that may be easily improved. Near this point is a tract of white pine, the first that is visible in ascending the St. Croix.

Pokeguma, twenty-five miles northwest from Sunrise, is noted as an old Indian missionary station.

Lake Superior is ninety-two miles from Taylor's Falls and one hundred and twenty from Stillwater.

CHAPTER XIII.

THE INTERIOR OF MINNESOTA, WATERED BY THE TRIBUTARIES OF THE MISSISSIPPI AND MISSOURI, AND BY NUMEROUS LAKES.—THE TOWNS OF FARIBAULT, FARMINGTON, LAKEVILLE, POPLAR GROVE, WATERFORD, MENDOTA, ROSE MOUNT, PILOT KNOB, ROCHESTER, CARMAN FALLS, ORONOCO, PLEASANT GROVE, CARIMONA, HAMILTON, CALEDONIA, HOKAH, HOUSTON CITY, ODESSA, AND ELLIOTA.—THE SOIL OF SOUTHERN MINNESOTA.

THE valleys of the Mississippi, Minnesota, and St. Croix, with the towns in each, having been described at as great length as the limits of a volnme of this size will permit, the next in order, to be brought before the reader, is the INTERIOR OF MINNESOTA TERRITORY.

From Stillwater via St. Anthony to the mouth of Redwood River, thence south to the Iowa line (the southern, if you please), thence east to the Mississippi, thence up the river to the place of beginning, you travel over a tract of land second to none in the northwest, in point of fertility, and which, as a general thing, is well supplied with timber and water. This Territory, bounded on the north by the Minnesota and on the north and east by the Mississippi, is watered by the Waraju, Wattonwon, Chanjuskah, Blue Earth, Tewapaden, Tankiyan, Tewapadan Psah, Le Seuer, Tchankiute, Owattanna, Chanjushkah, and other tributaries to the Minnesota. Besides all these, we have the Vermillion, Cannon, Zombra, Winneiska, Hokah, or Root River (each lying within the Territory), the Iowa, Red Cedar, and Des Moines, also having their sources in the Territory, and passing into Iowa. Independent of these streams and their numerous tributaries are a great many lakes, small and great, clear, beautiful, and healthful. The borders of the lakes differ as greatly in appearance as the lakes do in size. Some of them are surrounded by gentle grassy slopes, with occasional trees scattered along them, while others are bordered by extensive marshes, often overrun by the cranberry plant; again, the shores of some of them are abrupt, with a dense, dark forest skirting and overhanging their margins. Their beds are generally pebbly, or covered with small boulders; the water usually sweet and clear. Although a great number of lakes are shown on the maps of the Territory, but a very faint idea can be obtained therefrom of their number and location.

Although the region of country above referred to is rapidly filling up, there are as yet but few towns of importance. Nor dare I say which are now large or small, as the largest towns in the interior are less than a year old. Immigrants pour in by thousands, and where, but one short year ago, it was an unclaimed waste, cabins of settlers—actual tillers of the soil—men who came for the purpose of making the Territory a permanent home, and not merely for the purpose of securing a pre-emption—now arise in close proximity to each other, on every side, as far as the power of vision extends. Fine farms are being opened up, and, in another year, the first cabin of the settler will have been superseded by substantial and spacious farmhouses. Each of these districts must have a centre, and that centre will increase in population and importance in the same ratio as the surrounding country; hence the impossibility of judging of the size of towns after a temporary absence.

To describe the land in one portion of southern Minnesota is to describe it all. Except along the the bluffs next the river, or on the higher sandy divides between streams, the soil is very similar.

Faribault is pleasantly situated at the junction of Straight and Cannon Rivers, and is skirted on the east and south by beautiful groves of timber. General Shields states that, one year ago, there were but three buildings; now there are four sawmills in town, and twenty within ten miles. For one hundred days preceding the 1st of June, there had been erected one house per day. A Congregational church, with about thirty members, was organized here in May last

Farmington is situated on the Vermillion River, about fifteen miles from Hastings. This place is rightly named, for it looks like a village of farms. Good soil, good water, good timber, and intelligent citizens are its wealth.

Lakeville is situated on the Mendota and Big Sioux road, about twenty-five miles from Hastings. It takes its name from one of the loveliest bodies of water in the West. The lake forms nearly a circle, with a hard gravel beach throughout its whole circumference. The town is otherwise pleasantly located. Here are a good tavern, stores, and mechanic's shops.

Poplar Grove is a postal station, about seventeen miles from Hastings, near the Big Woods. There is timber in abundance and good farming land.

Waterford and Lewiston are situated on the Cannon River, and boast of as good a country as any of their neighbors.

Mendota is at the junction of the Minnesota and Mississippi Rivers. Its name is derived from the Sioux, and signifies a meeting of waters. Boats of the larger size can run to this point at all times of the year. It is at present the county-seat of Dacotah county. From Pilot Knob, back of Mendota, a view may be obtained of the country, eight or ten miles in extent, affording one of the most magnificent scenes in the Territory.

Rose Mount is a new post-office station just started on the Mendota and Big Sioux road, fourteen miles from Hastings; J. L. Turpin, P. M. Of the prairie on which the station is situated too much cannot be said. From one position we discovered twenty-one houses, where six months ago not more than two or three could be seen.

Rochester is situated in the centre of Olmstead county, at the great falls of the Zombro River. It is on the stage lines between Dubuque and St. Paul, and between Winona, St. Peters, and Mankato. Possessing a healthy location, good roads, fertile soil, and extensive water power, it would, under proper influences, succeed. Town proprietors should know that a dog-in-the-manger policy will retard the growth of a place, no matter what its advantages and attractions may be.

Cannon Falls, situated on a branch of the Cannon River, is growing rapidly, and promises to become a large manufacturing town. There is an abundance of water power, and the best of soil in every direction. A bridge, costing $3000, is being built over the Cannon River, between this place and Hastings.

Oronoco, in Olmstead county, is a brisk, new town, in a populous and rich agricultural district. The advantages claimed for this place are: first, its situation, in the centre of an excellent country, on the main thoroughfare from Dubuque to St. Paul, also on an air-line from Winona to Travese des Sioux. Second, its great mill privilege, having a water power limited only by the extent of improvement. And, third, the title is beyond a question. Aside from these, a grist-mill, saw-mill, plough factory, and an extensive brick-yard are in successful operation.

Pleasant Grove, in Olmstead county, is appropriately named, and will become an agricultural centre, but, I think, never a large town.

Carimona, on the south branch of Root River, the county-seat of Fillmore county, is supplied with flouring and saw-mills, good water power, with a fertile district surrounding.

Hamilton, in Fillmore county, is on the middle branch of Root River, fifteen miles southwest from Chatfield, and fifty from Winona, the nearest river point. Adjoining this village on the east is a body of timber, covering an area of about ten thousand acres. In the village are two fine large springs of the purest cold water, supplying a stream sufficient for a mill. Here is also a water privilege of fourteen feet fall, but partially employed. There are four mills (one grist) within five miles. This is a beautiful location, and is settled by Eastern people who term this the "New England Village."

Caledonia, the county-seat of Houston county is situated upon an elevated plateau of table land, high and gently rolling, requiring no grading at all, and affords an extensive view of the country adjoining; a profile of which would exhibit almost every variety of feature, and yet every foot of it may be cultivated.

Fears have been entertained, by persons travelling through northern Iowa and southern Minnesota, that it would be next to impossible to find water upon the elevated sites, so desirable for residences. Such has been the opinion formed of the location of Caledonia. A gentleman from that place informs us that a well was dug by Mr. S. McPhail, a few weeks ago; and, coming to water at a depth of twenty feet, it was walled up the same day within two feet of the top. It was noticed that the quantity of water running in continued to increase, and, on the following morning, it was *running over*, when it was found impossible to bail it out fast enough to enable the workmen to finish the wall!

Hokah is situated about six miles from Brownsville, on the Root River. A packet is probably running between this point and the Mississippi River. The Root River is navigable some fifteen miles.

Houston City is about fifteen miles from the Mississippi, on Root River, and is said to be a good location for a town. I did not visit it.

Chatfield, in Fillmore county, is the present location of the United States land office of the Root River district. The travel through and business in the place, together with its natural advantages, are building up a town here with a rapidity known only in the West.

Oakland and Mantorville, in Dodge county, are

beautifully and advantageously located towns, and worthy the attention of new-comers.

The face of the country near the Mississippi is somewhat broken and uneven, covered with good timber for farming purposes, and irrigated with springs of pure soft water, gushing from the hills, forming brooks which are literally alive with the finest trout. The soil of these hills has proved to be well adapted to winter wheat, and the valleys produce heavy crops of corn.

Back from the river the country gradually becomes more level, and the western half of the river counties is composed of fine rolling prairie, interspersed with groves, and generally well watered. The soil of these prairies equals the best of Illinois for the culture of corn, and far excels in small grains. Winter wheat is considered a sure crop.

Odessa is situated at the junction of Iowa River and the boundary line, on the line between ranges 10 and 11; and is one of the most go-ahead places in southern Minnesota. The place is quite new, has most excellent water power, and is a good point for manufactories.

I but speak the sentiments of every visitor, when I say, that southern Minnesota has lost nothing in my estimation by an enlarged acquaintance. It can but be considered as a certainty that nearly, if not quite, all of the towns now located on the stage road from Dubuque to St. Paul will soon become important central points of business for the large tracts of country by which they are severally surrounded. The amount of freight and the number of passengers now being carried over that great thoroughfare is immense, for a new country, and is increasing in a wonderful ratio. Rochester, Pleasant Grove, Jordan, Fillmore, Carimona, Waukokee, and Elliota, on the Iowa State line, can each share in the business thus afforded, without interfering with the prosperity of the other. With direct communications to Eastern markets, manufacturing facilities, and locations in the heart of one of the best agricultural countries in the West, their future growth is not a matter of speculation, but a fixed fact.

CHAPTER XIV.

TRIP FROM WINONA TO SIOUX CITY.—SOUTH BEND AND THE COUNTRY NORTH.—NEW ULM, GLENCOE HUTCHINSON, CEDAR CITY, CAMDEN, RAPID WATER, FREMONT, HIGH ISLAND, GRIMSHAW, GREENWOOD, FOREST CITY, EXCELSIOR.—THE COUNTRY BETWEEN THE UPPER MISSISSIPPI AND THE UPPER MINNESOTA.

A CORRESPONDENT of the Red Wing Sentinel thus speaks of his tour from Red Wing to Sioux City:

"Between Owatonia and Verona, on the Blue Earth, the country is fast filling up. There are Wilton, on the Le Sueur; Chambers' Settlement in the Cobb; a short distance from thence, a settlement on the Minnesota Lake, township 104 north, range 25 west. West of Minnesota Lake, eight miles, on Maple River, is a good settlement (Fogg's). From thence to Verona, in township 103 north, range 27 west, are settlements, with accessions daily. From Verona to the Iowa State line, where the Sioux City and the Mendota military road strikes the State line, between ranges 32 and 33 west, a distance of thirty or thirty-five miles, are various settlements — Bigelow's, five miles from Verona; Weller's, Mead's, Rogers', and Baitts', on the Chain Lakes, in townships 101 and 102 north, ranges 29 and 30; from Baitts' to Tuttle's, or Tuttle's Lake, 12 miles; from Tuttle's to the point where the military road first touches the State line, six miles (from this point the military road follows the State line to 35 west). From Tuttle's to the Des Moines River is about twelve miles.

"The road from Fort Dodge to Fort Ridgely passes at an equal distance between Tuttle's and Des Moines. From the point in 35 west, where the military road finally leaves the State line, to the country in and about Spirit Lake, a distance of about ten or twelve miles, the settlements are of recent date, but with the prospect of a heavy addition before another month. From Spirit Lake, through Dickson, O'Brien, and Plymouth counties, to Sioux City, crossing the head waters of Little Sioux, thence to the head of Floyd's River and down that stream, a good road can be had through a settled country.

"At Spirit Lake the nearest post-offices are Fort Dodge and Mankato — distance about seventy miles. By fall, there will be a necessity for offices on an average of about every ten miles. We need a mail route from Red Wing, via Owatonia, Milton, and Verona, crossing the Des Moines at some point on Spirit Lake, to form a junction there with the St. Paul and Sioux City road. Our road is more practicable than the military road, even when $8,000 shall have been spent on it.

"Emigration is approaching the Mississippi from an unusual source. Emigrants landing at Sioux City are looking for land on the Big Sioux, Floyd's, Des Moines, and even Blue Earth Rivers.

"The country west of the Des Moines, on and near the State line, is well watered with streams connecting various lakes. The land is rich, and in many places covered with a beautiful growth of red top grass, constituting one of the best agricultural and stock-raising countries in the world. The objection is a scarcity of timber. In some places there is a sufficiency, in others an abundance; but, taking the country broadcast, there is a deficiency, and this constitutes the only objection.

"We need some connection with the country on the Missouri, by means of roads, mail routes, etc.; and, when this is done, our business relations will spring up. At Sioux City, pine lumber is $100 per thousand feet; shingles, $15 per thousand; cotton-wood lumber, $40 per thousand feet. Some there are who talk of steamboating lumber up the Minnesota as far as practicable, hauling it from thence to the Jaques, and floating it down to Sioux City. *That is a project!* A railroad is just the thing. We could furnish lumber, and that coal. A coal bank is being opened at Sergeant's Bluffs, eight miles below Sioux City.

"At present, our nearest communication with the Missouri will be by way of Sioux City, on account of the intervening Indian lands between it and the Big Sioux on the west. At present, they cannot even be explored. These unceded lands are but little occupied by the Indians, but one evidence of an old camp being seen from the mouth of Big Sioux to the Territorial line. Immigrants are even at this time anxiously waiting at Sioux City, in hopes of the speedy cession of these lands.

"We are directly interested in extinguishing the Indian titles. The recent appropriation by Congress for the road from Fort Ridgely to the South Pass will be expended in vain, if the country through which the road passes is not thrown open to the pioneer. I know that this tract is said to be *worthless*, but a peep into the promised lands has a tendency to render those sceptical who have been thus favored."

Blue Earth City, the county-seat of Faribault county, was organized in February last, and is located upon a charming plateau, in the forks of the Blue Earth River. Immigrants are already rapidly settling the town and county.

Garden City, on the Wattonwon, is a new town just "rounding into form." It is situated where a town is much wanted, in order to supply the rich agricultural district surrounding. It is about eight miles south of South Bend, having a lovely site, and located in a district thickly settled by the very best class of people. From its water power and other advantages, I anticipate a large town here at an early day.

From here, we pass to South Bend, another point that nature has doubtless marked out for a large town. Everything seems favorable, except the lack of capital and citizens. This section — the south bend of the Minnesota and the Blue Earth country — is attracting more attention from all classes of settlers and capitalists than probably any other one point in the Territory.

The north side of the Minnesota is also a splendid country, studded with numerous towns, which are worthy of note.

New Union, the county-seat of Brown county, is located twenty-five miles above St. Peter, and one degree farther south than St. Paul. Within a year, nearly two hundred families, principally German and Swiss, have located here. The "German Land Company" are the original proprietors of this region. This company was organized some years ago at Chicago, and is here operating much upon the plan of the "building associations" of large cities. This place is ten miles below Fort Ridgely, embracing a beautiful section of country; and, with the efforts now being put forth, we shall soon see "the wilderness blossom as the rose."

Glencoe is the county-seat of McLeod county, and is located at the edge of what is known as "the great northwest prairie." This place is attracting considerable attention, which it richly deserves. Although this section is very rapidly settling, there were still claims to be made on eligible and desirable sites, within a few miles of Glencoe. This place is in township 115, range 21 west. High-Island Lake, seven miles distant, is a beautiful sheet of water. The country around it, as well as that of Lake Adda, twelve miles distant, and that near the Minnesota, is the best of farming land.

Hutchinson is the name of the new town located by the Hutchinson family — Asa, John, and Judson, of singing notoriety — on the middle fork of Crow River, which they have named Hassan River. This place is seventeen miles northwest of Glencoe, surrounded by an abundance of timber and prairie, and supplied with good water power. This will be one of the largest inland towns north of the Minnesota.

Cedar City is in township 117, range 29 west, on the bank of the beautiful Red Cedar Lake. This place is thirty miles northwest of Glencoe. The immigrant will here find hard-wood timber land and beautiful rolling prairies, waiting to be claimed and settled.

Camden is situated at the junction of Buffalo Creek with Hassan River, on the new Territorial road from Lake Minnetouka to Glencoe. It is distant from Glencoe twelve miles, and thirty from St. Anthony.

Rapid Water is on the south fork of Crow River, in section 4, township 117, range 25 west.

Fremont is situated in section 28, township 117 range 28, on that charming lakelet, Silver Lake. This town is new, thrifty, and inviting.

High Island is on a lake of the same name, eight miles south of Glencoe, near the border of and within Sibley county.

Grimshaw Settlement, on Lake Adda, in section 21, township 115, range 29, is twelve miles west of Glencoe.

Greenwood is situated at the forks of Crow River, in sections 30 and 31, township 119, range 24, distant from St. Paul thirty miles, and from Shakopee twenty-three miles. This site is a verdant spot, selected by an old Indian trader of keen perception, good judgment, and an experience of years in the Territory. Nothing but mechanics and capital are needed to make this a first-class town. The legislature, at its last session, incorporated this place as *a city!* To give some idea of the growth of this country, I will state that, one year ago, Mr. Allen, one of the proprietors of Greenwood, came through from Lake Minnetouka, and "blazed his way" with a butcher knife. On this trail there is now a Territorial road, and every claim on it is taken. On almost every one is a comfortable log cabin, and on some of them neat-looking framed houses are being built. Then there was no road coming here. Now territorial roads are located from Shakopee and Minneapolis, and others are legalized from Monticello, Anoka, and Forest City.

Then one hastily built cabin was all that there was of this now flourishing village — *city*, I should say!

Forest City is situated in a central point, at the foot of the rapids on the north fork of Crow River, the best water power to be found on the waters of that extensive stream, draining, as it does, a large region of country, comprising the richest prairies and timbered districts Minnesota can boast of. The people of Monticello, Clearwater, and St. Cloud are now briskly employed in reaching this fertile centre of farming lands, and seem to be engaged in a laudable emulation to see who can do most to help the industrious immigrant to this inland paradise. The county commissioners met on the first Monday of May, and organized the county, pursuant to law, by the appointment of a sheriff, register of deeds, etc., whilst the company are engaged in building a saw-mill, hotel, and other public conveniences.

The farmer or immigrant can hardly go amiss anywhere in this section, between the Upper Mississippi and the Upper Minnesota. The last legislature appointed commissioners to establish roads to Forest City from Minneapolis, from Shakopee, via Greenwood, from Monticello, and from St. Cloud.

Excelsior has recently been staked off, and the town site was entered in May last, situated on sections 27, 34, and 35, in township 117, range 23.

These towns are all beautifully and advantageously situated in a fertile section of country. That immigrants may the more readily find the locations, while travelling over the country, I have given the section, township, and range of the smaller towns; for some of them, though large and populous, are not shown upon the map, so recent has been their organization and so rapid their growth.

CHAPTER XV.

LIFE IN THE WEST. — EASTERN ERRORS CORRECTED. — WESTERN MEN. — HOW WESTERN CITIES ARE MADE. — GROWTH OF THE WEST. — "OVERWROUGHT REPRESENTATIONS" OF THE WEST.

VERY few Eastern people have a correct conception of Western society, or the rapid progress of the West. The exultant "Eureka" springs to the lips of the wanderer from boyhood's Eastern home, when he treads the horizon-bound prairie, or roams along the banks of our lakes and rivers; but it dies away unuttered as he mingles in our society, or compares our works of improvement with the time in which they have been accomplished; for then his soul is filled with emotions of wonder and surprise to find that our valley is so unlike what his day-dream fancies had painted it. The prairie, with its rich soil and profuse vegetation — a wide expanse of natural garden plot — is like what he had conceived; the forests, the rivers, the lakes, the mounds, these are somewhat like his fanciful ideas; but the character of our people, and the works they have performed, are totally unlike all that the generality of Eastern people have imagined.

In emigrating to the West, men have come here, not to be conquered by nature, but to make her lavish bounty subservient to their wants and aspirations. Therefore, in our Western homes, idleness, or vulgarity, or ignorance, are rarely met. The father remembers the gentle courtesy, that gave such a charm to the social intercourse which had made his early years a long season of almost undisturbed happiness; he remembers how, in his former home, the priceless boon of education raised men far above the level; he looks forward to the coming time, when his children will jostle through a crowded city, or dwell in the country whose every acre of rich soil shall yield to industry its meet reward — and he builds a school-house, patronizes booksellers and printers, and introduces into his family the refining influences that endear to his memory his old home. The mother has like hopes in the future of the West, shares in her husband's wishes, and encourages and aids him. Thus it is that pleasure, comfort, and intelligence — free, perhaps, from many of the restraints of Eastern life — are almost invariably to be found in Western homes.

In Western life, the trials and obstacles endured by the early settler aroused his dormant energies, and he became active and persevering. Nature repays his toils with abundant harvests, and his heart warms with gratitude and grows great with generous impulses. Around him, cities, villages, manufactories, and farm-houses are built up with a rapidity rivalling the fabulous wonders of the "Arabian Nights;" and he drinks in large draughts of the spirit of enterprise which does all this. He sees men whom he knew in the East as only "nobodies," aspiring to be "somebodies" in the West —heading the van of political parties, boldly debating in the councils of the people, vigorously laboring to advance new and gigantic enterprises — and he forms a more exalted and correct estimate of mankind. Perhaps he grows ambitious too, and endeavors himself to become a leader, instead of a follower. He tills with his own hands more acres than his father owned, he gathers larger crops than they did, he has brighter anticipations, of the future, and all his ideas, sentiments, and impulses, are in proportion vivified and enlarged. And thus it is that Western people become energetic, persevering, enterprising, ambitious, and generous, in the extreme.

In the union of these characteristics in our people lies the true secret of the rapid progress of our country, and the West generally, which is greater and more widely extended than Eastern people believe.

The sun goes down at night, casting his last rays upon the lingering form of the Indian journeyer to the farther west. As it rises in the morning, its beams flash back from the axe of the white man, as he shapes the rude logs which are to form

his habitation. A few days pass on, and then the curling smoke rolls up from the fire of the first settler. Through the long winter he plies his axe; and, when spring birds begin to carol, their music is drowned by the buzz of the saw-mill. Summer passes, and when winter comes again, new dwellings surround the house of the first pioneer, and more axe-strokes than his ring through the forest.

Again spring returns, and with it come new settlers, to live with the lumberman and his family—the tailor, the shoemaker, and the dress-maker to clothe them; the grocery-keeper and the merchant to supply their wants; the farmer to raise their grain; the schoolmaster to teach their children; the minister to preach to and counsel and advise with them; the doctor to cure them when sick; the lawyer to settle or make their difficulties. Then the settlement has become a village—not an Eastern one, but a wide awake, go-ahead, Western *village.* The newspaper soon makes its first appearance; the editor talks largely of the prospects of the village, and of the agricultural and lumbering country around it, and proposes more improvements to the village in any one number of his paper than would be sufficient to paralyze a Down-East community. Adventurers push out into the country, pick out more locations and build up more villages. More farmers and lumbermen come into the country. The lumbering business makes a ready market for the farmer's produce, while the lumbermen's commodities are more than sufficient to supply the home demand, and "ten-acre" rafts are run down the river to the large cities below.

Perhaps, at the time when the first pioneer was erecting his log cabin, in some farm-house or in the attic of some city boarding-house, "away Down East," sits one who has a map before him. He sticks a pin in some particular point, and tries to judge whether it would be a good place for him to select for his Western home. He inquires of travelers, and reads newspapers, to learn what he can of the country. Two or three years pass before he fairly makes up his mind, and then he starts for the West. When he reaches the point he had selected, great is his surprise to find villages and cultivated fields all around him, and that the West of which he has dreamed, and the hardships which he has come prepared to meet, are still a far-off land. He finds that his home is to be where he can enjoy all the comforts, and meet with all the refinements, of the East — among a people whom he cannot but admire, and whose peculiarities will soon be his own. He gains a freedom that he could not have experienced in the East; his labor is repaid better than it was there. His mind every day comes in contact with the quick and strong intellect which characterizes Western people, and receives its natural polish and elasticity. He gains in health, because the air is pure and bracing;

mind and body are exercised equally and properly; he laughs heartily occasionally, and is always light-hearted. Then the man is a man indeed. Intellectually and physically invigorated, he becomes one of the most useful men of the age — *a Western man!*

You think, perhaps, that Western people are extravagant in praising up the many attractions of life in the West, and of boasting of their own works; yet all of us were Eastern people but a few years since, and thought of the West as you do now, that it was the place to make money, but not the place to live. What Eastern man is there among your list of acquaintances, who has come to the West, and upon whose veracity and judgment you can rely, who did not write back to his friends that life had new charms for him, and that the West appeared as though the most extravagant descriptions fell far short of the reality? If we boast of our own works of improvement in the West, have we not on every hand a thousand proofs to sustain us? The former wild prairie, now a cultivated farm; the floating palaces upon the bosom of the river which but a little while ago rolled on undisturbed in its lonely beauty; the churches and school-houses that now stand where stood a few summers since the Indian's wigwam; the steam-cars, that fly across the land swifter than the light-footed Chippewa, the arrow from his bow, or the deer that he hunted, — are not all these proofs enough that we are justified in boasting of what we have accomplished? If you think not, go do as much as we have done, and refrain from boasting, if you can. — *North Star.*

CHAPTER XVI.

IMMIGRATION INTO THE NORTHWEST.—WHAT HAS CAUSED THIS GREAT COMMOTION.—EXTRACTS FROM THE PRESS.

For the past twelve or fifteen years there has been a large annual emigration from the Eastern States, and latterly the Middle States, to the northern half of the Mississippi Valley; and, instead of decreasing, the tide of emigration appears to be continually swelling. This year, as we learn from the New England journals, the number of emigrants westward will fully equal that of 1855, if not exceed it. The constantly improving and extending facilities offered to travelers have their influence in inducing the inhabitants of the mountainous regions of the East to seek a more agreeable home in the fertile valleys and rich mineral districts of the West. The more accurate knowledge of the western country, the salubrity of the climate, and the civilization of the inhabitants, which has to a great extent superseded the former ridiculous impressions in relation to everything western, will also tend to increase the number of western home-seekers. These, and other influences, together with that mysterious desire for change—in both senses of the word—which is said to be a prominent characteristic of the Yankee, will co-operate to cause a large influx of Eastern men into the Western States during this and many succeeding years. I can in no better way illustrate this immense immigration, than by inserting extracts from a few of the newspapers of the Territory. The St. Paul Pioneer says: "No adequate idea of the almost miraculous settlement of the country can be formed by our citizens, unless they are in the habit of visiting the country surrounding us frequently during the spring and summer months. Immigrants pour in by thousands, and where, but one short year ago, it was an unclaimed waste, now cabins of settlers—actual tillers of the soil—men who came for the purpose of making the Territory a permanent home, and not merely for the purpose of securing a pre-emption, arise in close proximity to each other, on every side, as far as the power of vision extends. Instead of thousands of acres remaining unclaimed, not a single acre can be found but what has an owner; and instead of a few detached 'claim shanties,' the prairie is now thickly dotted with them, and, in many instances, although not a year has elapsed since the date of their settlement, neat and commodious frame houses have been erected by the settlers. Instead of an uncultivated waste, now on every hand can be seen fields of all the cereal grains, potatoes, corn, and, in short, every article of produce usually raised by the farmers in the States.

"This is not the history of a single settlement. It is the same throughout the Territory. Everywhere, go where you will, you will find a constant stream of immigrants coming into the country from every part of the Union, who have been attracted hither by the salubrity of our climate, the productiveness of the soil, and the facilities for obtaining a homestead."

The Henderson Democrat says: "It is astonishing how fast the claims are taken up in the country back, on both sides of the river. On the east side of the river excellent claims could be found within three miles of the river a few weeks ago, but they are now taken and occupied by actual settlers. Immigrants, on the look-out for locations, are traversing every part of the country, and even the poorest pieces are being improved. The immense influx of immigrants into this section of the valley is surprising, and the number seems to increase constantly. No greedy speculators can ever prey upon the community, and grow and fatten upon the energy and enterprise of the actual settlers. Every one hundred and sixty acres will have on it a producer and consumer — a producer of the products of the farm, and a consumer of merchandize and mechanical work.

"No vast tracts of country will lie unimproved and unproductive, because they are beyond the reach of those who would make them yield rich harvests, and cover them with cheerful homes, benefiting both themselves and society."

The St. Peter Courier, of June last, says: "From forty to fifty immigrant teams have crossed our ferry the past week; and, in addition to this, scores of families are arriving every week by other routes.

"On yesterday morning two more colonies arrived —one bound for Crow River, the other for Rum River. They brought with them their cattle and horses, and all the paraphernalia of farmers."— *St Paul Democrat.*

The Cleveland Plaindealer says: "Never before in the history of the country has the tide of emigration from the East to the Westward been so fast and furious."

The rapid settlement of the country between Hastings and Faribault may be learned from the following memorandum of the travel in and out on the Cannon River road, in one day, viz.: Double teams, 149; single buggies, 14; stages, 2; yokes of cattle, 14.

I will conclude with a word or two from the Eastern press.

The Bennington (Vermont) State Banner says: "Some twenty, mostly from Washington, took the cars at this place during the week, destined for that 'garden of Eden,' where the 'land flows with milk and honey'—where a man has but to 'open wide his mouth' to have it 'filled with the finest of wheat.' Nothing but a parcel of 'old fogies' will be found in Vermont five years hence. The prospect for a young man here, unless he chances to be 'born with a silver spoon in his mouth,' is anything but flattering. He can, if he toils early and late, and eats the bread of carefulness, possibly keep soul and body together, and keep himself and family from becoming inmates of the town farm. But this will not at all satisfy the 'Young America' spirit of the age, and they will never rest easy under such an arrangement. There are plenty of homes in the West, and thither our young men, accompanied by their young and beautiful 'help-meets,' are rapidly hastening. Success to them. May they even reap more of earth's bounties and blessings than ever imagination has pictured before their anxious eyes, or their joyous hearts had ever anticipated."

The N. Y. Independent says: "Probably not less than a quarter of a million of people will emigrate the present year to our frontier States and Territories. Never was there such excitement on the subject before. It pervades all classes, in every city, town, and village. Students in colleges, professional, business men—the most talented in all quarters—are taking possession of the soil, as a surer foundation for permanent prosperity than can be found in any other vocation. What a glorious spectacle, and how promising the future! Let it be praised and encouraged, as the surest policy to promote our growth, strength, and high elevation.

"The Stafford Western Emigration Company, comprising from 600 to 700 persons, of all ages and both sexes, including from 100 to 200 from the city of Lowell, are to start soon for the 'Far West.' The New York and Erie Railroad Company will forward this large party, in detachments, as far as Dubuque, Iowa, at which point the locating committee will make known the site selected for the settlement of the colony. The company is composed of some very substantial New England men, who have already paid to their treasurer $20,000."

The New Hampshire Patriot of a late date says: "We hear of persons in all sections of the State, who are starting for the West, or are preparing to go, while many have already gone this spring. In one day last week, an agent on one of the great routes to the West sold fifteen tickets to men going from this vicinity. There is no doubt that more people will leave this State for the West this year than have gone in any past three years."

Immense Foreign Emigration Threatened.— We see, by a letter from the London correspondent of the National Intelligencer, that most extensive preparations are being made to facilitate emigration from Germany, on a larger scale than ever before. This will no doubt enable Roman Catholicism to further its views in relation to the government of this country. The immigration for the past year was 470,000, exclusive of those who came by the way of Nova Scotia and the Canadas. Taking these into account, it will not be less than half a million. Yet in the present year we are to have a still larger immigration.

"A steamer, with one hundred and fifty German immigrants, from Bremen, arrived at St. Louis recently. They were on their route to Iowa and Minnesota, and since they left Bremen eleven children have been born to them."

The Lansingburg (N. Y.) Gazette says: "The other morning we missed the peculiar ring of our milkman's bells, substituted by a tinkle on another key. 'Where is Peter Ham?' we asked of the stranger. 'He 's sold to me and gone West,' was the response.

"A day or two since we stopped at the fence of Mr. Lea's garden. 'Where is Mr. Lea?' we asked of one of his family. 'Prospecting out West.'—'Is Mr. Charles Hitchcock in?'—'No, sir, he 's out West.'—'I shall move first of May,' says Andrew Derrick.—'Where?'—'Out West.' And so we might go on to the end of the chapter.

"Why, 'land of goodness,' as the old woman said, what is to become of us, at this rate? Such an exodus was never known in our town. We hope there will enough remain to bury those who can't get away."

CHAPTER XVII.

PUBLIC LANDS IN MINNESOTA. — SALES THEREOF IN 1855. — PRE-EMPTIONS. — LAND SUBJECT TO PRE-EMPTION.

The amount of land entered in the land offices in this Territory, prior to the first of January, 1855, was as follows:

	Whole No. of acres.	Located by Warrants.	Amount received in cash.
Stillwater,	400,709 52	158,528 18	$302,482 80
Sauk Rapids,	31,507 59	4,600 00	33,634 48
Root River,	82,414 07	1,960 00	103,018 12
Minneapolis,	12,876 04	2,151 00	16,093 81
Total,	527,607 22	167,239 18	$455,229 21

1855.

	Whole No. of acres.	Located by Warrants.	Amount received in cash.
Stillwater,	180,413 80	56,484 85	$154,861 83
Sauk Rapids,	64,499 50	19,609 00	56,692 15
Root River,	243,465 04	81,580 00	304,332 91
Minneapolis,	137,195 80	8,609 00	183,677 17
Winona,	218,266 37	47,340 00	218,527 12
Red Wing,	196,390 69	43,068 00	204,572 99
Total.			
Sales in 1855,	1,040,231 20	256,781 85	$1,122,844 17
Prior to 1855,	527,607 22	167,239 18	455,229 21
Total.	1,567,838 42	424,020 93	$1,578,073 38

"In the history of the country, we do not think such a record as the above can be found. In one year, the United States received from the sales of public lands in this Territory, over $1,000,000; and in addition, we find that, in 1855, 256,781 acres of land warrants, donated by the General Government to old soldiers and modern speculators, as a reward for the bravery of one class in the service of their country, and the zeal displayed by the other species in beseiging Congress, were located in Minnesota. By placing the Government valuation upon this land, we find that the total value of the land disposed of in 1855, in this Territory, amounts to the sum of $1,443,823, and since 1848, to $2,108,100.

We do not think any State or Territory in the Union can exhibit such substantial marks of progress during the year 1855 as the above indicates. It will be perceived that the sales of land during that year doubled the entire amount disposed of during the preceding seven years, and that the receipts into the United States Treasury, for lands disposed of during 1855, amounted to nearly treble that of the previous seven years.

"We do not claim the sales of 1855 as having been made exclusively to the settlers of that year. Far from it. There was no land office west of the Mississippi in this Territory until 1854, and settlers poured into that fertile portion of Minnesota as soon as the treaty, by which the Indians ceded it to the General Government, was ratified. But that the population of the west side more than doubled in 1855 we firmly believe; and if one-half of the sales made during the year are awarded to the settlers of that year, we do not think the estimate will be extravagant.

"PRE-EMPTIONS IN 1855.—The number of pre-emptions granted to actual settlers is a fair indication of the prosperity and growth of a new country. This proposition, which no one will dispute, places Minnesota at the head of the States and Territories of the Union, in the rapidity with which it is being settled. The records of the general land office at Washington bear witness to the fact, that the number of patents granted for lands pre-empted in Minnesota exceeds the whole number of patents granted to the remaining Territories and States of the Union. The settlement of no State in the confederacy can parallel this unexampled growth!

"It is extremely difficult to obtain the figures showing the amount of the pre-emption business in 1855. The land officers, in their reports, merely gave us the amount of land entered under the pre-emption act of 1841, during the year.

"In the Sauk Rapids district, during the year, five thousand four hundred and twenty-seven acres were entered by pre-emption.

"In the Red Wing District, one hundred and

forty-four thousand and five acres were sold by pre-emption.

"In the Winona district, one thousand and sixty-three pre-emptions were allowed, covering one hundred and forty-nine thousand nine hundred and seventy-nine acres. This would make an average of one hundred and forty-one acres to each pre-emptor.

"In the Minneapolis district, the number of pre-emptions allowed since the establishment of the office, in 1854, to the end of 1855, was one thousand and sixty-six. All but four of these pre-emptions were made on twelve fractional townships, containing, in round numbers, one hundred and sixty thousand acres. In the month of October, five hundred and twenty-five pre-emptions were allowed at the Minneapolis office.

"In the Stillwater district, during 1854, one thousand three hundred and eight acres were entered under the pre-emption law of 1841.

"In the Brownsville district, one hundred and twenty-six thousand four hundred and seventy-nine acres were entered by pre-emption.

"The above statement shows that in 1855, more than one-half of the land sold in Minnesota was disposed of under the beneficial workings of the pre-emption law of 1841."

"Lands subject to Entry and to Pre-Emption. — In the Stillwater and Sauk Rapids districts, previous to the proclamation of the President in the fall of 1855, there was land subject to private entry at the land offices; but, in the four districts west of the river, there was no land subject to private entry until after the public sales of October and November last.

"There was, on the first day of January, subject to private entry, the following amount of land at the different offices in the Territory; at the Stillwater land office, 691,200 acres; Sauk Rapids, 483,840; Brownsville, 691,200; Minneapolis, 2,637; Winona, 63,000; Red Wing, 20,000.

"This amount has been materially diminished since the first of January. At all the offices, since that time, land has been entered by the settlers and speculators, in considerable quantities.

"In all the districts there is a vast amount of land subject to pre-emption under the provisions of the act of 1841. At the Stillwater office, on the first of January, there were fourteen townships subject to pre-emption; and the land officers had been notified by the department, that the plats of thirty-six townships would shortly be returned. Of this land, much of it is valuable farming land in the vicinity of Rum River. In the Sauk Rapids district, twenty-two townships have been surveyed, and are open to pre-emption. In the Brownsville district, there are one hundred and twenty-four townships subject to pre-emption. The surveys in this district have been prosecuted one hundred and seventy-five miles west of the Mississippi. In the Minneapolis district, on the first of January, there were but three townships subject to pre-emption. Since that time, plats of other townships have been returned. In the Winona district, there are two million acres subject to pre-emption, and in the Red Wing district, one million acres." *

LATER. — The register of the Minneapolis district gives the following statistics for the six months ending the 1st of July, 1856: pre-empted, 63,015 acres; entered, 1,703; subject to entry, about 900 acres.

In the Stillwater land office, during the month of June, the sales of public lands were as follows: For cash, 7,281 35 acres, valued at $9,101 69; for warrants, 134,671 24 acres, valued at $168,339 05; total, 141,952 59 acres, valued at $177,440 74. The sales for July averaged about 5000 acres per day.

* For these valuable statistics, we are indebted to the editor of the St. Paul Pioneer and Democrat.

CHAPTER XVIII.

BOUNDARY AND DESCRIPTION OF LAND DISTRICTS, AND CHARACTER OF THE SETTLERS.—NEW LAND DISTRICTS, ETC.

STILLWATER LAND DISTRICT.—The Sauk Rapids and Stillwater districts comprise all the lands east of the Mississippi in Minnesota; but, by the provisions of the act of 1854, creating new land districts in Minnesota, the Sauk Rapids district was extended west of the Mississippi, taking in five townships fronting on the river, and running west to the "Drift Wood," and the Red River of the North.

In answer to an inquiry in reference to the character of the population in this district, Mr. Holcomb writes that, "in a business sense, they are an enterprising business people; and, to justify this conclusion, I will state some facts. In this district there are saw-mills that saw an entire log by once running through, and so arranged, that one log follows another continuously, without loss of time. At one of the mills, a circular saw, for making flooring and fencing, cuts both ways; that is, as the carriage moves one way, the saw cuts in its downward motion, and as it returns, the saw cuts on the opposite side, in its upward motion. Besides these, we have machines for planing, flooring and siding, making shingles, lath, doors, sash, wagons, sleighs, etc., to which I may add, the large and increasing business of logging in the pineries. It has been estimated that one hundred million feet of pine lumber, in the log, were put into the different streams in this district, within the present year, which, at $10 per thousand feet, the estimated value, amounts to $1,000,000. Interspersed through the entire pine country are excellent lands for agriculture, in good proportions, so that the $1,000,000 annual resources from the pine is so much in addition to the resources of an *exclusively agricultural district*, and harmonizes well as a basis for a home market.

Sauk Rapids District. — The country lying on the Mississippi, above the falls, though unequalled in fertility and natural advantages, has not increased so rapidly in population and wealth as the southern portion of the Territory. The reason for this is obvious; and is to be found in the fact that the upper country has been without the proper means of affording the immigrant a speedy and cheap conveyance to its fertile prairies and beautiful wood-lands. Boats are now running from St. Anthony to Sauk Rapids, as also a regular line of stages. A road has been constructed from the west end of Lake Superior to the Mississippi, and it is not improbable that a large immigration will be diverted to Benton and the surrounding counties, by the Lake Superior route, during the coming summer.

Mr. Woods also sets down the increase of his district, in population, at one hundred per cent. He says of the population, that they are "industrious, enterprising, and money-making."

Of the lands in the Sauk Rapids district that remain subject to private entry, a great proportion consists of good farming land, well watered, and eligibly situated. Much choice prairie land near the Mississippi River remains yet subject to private entry. This land makes excellent farms with comparatively little labor, and wood for building and fencing can always be secured within a reasonable distance.

The Sauk River valley, on the west side of the Mississippi River, is now being rapidly settled by an industrious and enterprising population, and is destined to become one of the most populous and wealthy, as well as most attractive, valleys in Minnesota. Many large farms are already under cultivation, and the yield of wheat, oats, and potatoes is such as could hardly be expected even from the fertile bottoms of Illinois. This beautiful valley is yet unsurveyed, but is *claimed* and occupied for many miles along the banks of Sauk River — more than twenty — west from its mouth.

Lying upon the Mississippi, there are in the district immense pineries, commencing at the mouth of Crow Wing River, and extending for more than fifty miles northward, along the bank of the Mississippi, and many miles back. Besides this vast pinery, much valuable pine land is found on Rum, Platte, and Long Prairie Rivers. Eight saw-mills are in operation within the district.

Root River Land District. — This district comprises a favorite portion of Minnesota, and one which, as the tabular statements exhibit, has more rapidly increased in population during 1855 than any other portion of the Territory. In the Root River district, there are at present, subject to pre-emption, lands in the counties of Fillmore, Mower, Freeborn, Faribault, and in the southern tier of townships in Olmstead, Dodge, Steele, and Blue Earth counties. For fertility, these lands are not exceeded by any on the continent.

Mr. M'Kenny estimates that the rate of increase in population, in the Brownsville district, during 1855, has been *five hundred per cent;* and, judging from personal observation, and conversations with gentlemen who have had every opportunity of acquiring truthful information, we think this estimate a small one, rather than extravagant.

The population of the Chatfield district consists principally of emigrants from the States of New York, Massachusetts, Connecticut, Vermont, Pennsylvania, Ohio, Michigan, Indiana, Illinois, Wisconsin, and Iowa. There are several extensive settlements of Norwegians in this district, as well as German, Irish, Scotch, Swedes, and Canadians. As to the character of these settlers, they are an intelligent and industrious people. This district, in common with the others created by the law of 1854, is thirty miles wide north and south, and extends west from the Mississippi River to the Big Sioux River. The southern line of the district is the boundary line between Minnesota and Iowa.

MINNEAPOLIS LAND DISTRICT. — The Minneapolis district extends west from the Mississippi River to the line of the Sioux reservation which runs from the Big Sioux River to Lac Traverse.

The settlements in this district have advanced far beyond the surveys, and the land officers estimate the increase of population at *four hundred per cent.*

The settlers in this district are farmers; industrious, thrifty, moral, and intelligent. About two-thirds of them are Americans by birth, and the rest are Irish, Germans, and Canadian French, in about equal proportions.

The country between the Minnesota and Mississippi, situated in this district, is very fertile, and in its wild state presents a beautiful appearance. Rolling prairies, dotted with small lakes of clear water, and orchard-like groves of trees, are the principal characteristics of the scenery. Many thriving inland villages are springing up, while the farming population is increasing at a rapid rate.

WINONA LAND DISTRICT.— This district is thirty miles wide from north to south, and extends west from the Mississippi to the Big Sioux River. There are in this district nearly two millions of acres subject to pre-emption, including as choice agricultural lands as the most theoretical or practical farmer could desire. It is mostly prairie, interspersed with groves of timber, watered by numerous springs, rivulets, and rivers, which abound in speckled trout and others of the finny tribes (listen, ye disciples of the good Izaak Walton!), and affording, in their course to the Father of Waters, numerous water powers, capable of easy improvement.

In speaking of the population of this district, Mr. L. D. Smith, the receiver at the land office at Winona, says, that, "in point of intelligence, perseverance, and every qualification going to make up an enlightened and prosperous community, they will compare favorably with any other class of persons that he has ever seen."

The great majority of the settlers are from the States — New York having contributed much the largest number. There are two or three settlements of Norwegians in this district, and Scotland has its representatives in a few localities; while, from different parts of the district, the "sweet German accent and the rich Irish brogue" are frequently heard.

The increase of population in the district for the year 1855 has been at least five hundred per cent, which, to some, may appear incredible, though Mr. Smith is satisfied that the facts will fully sustain the assertion. To show the rapid increase in that portion of Minnesota, he instances the county of Olmsted. In what is now Olmsted county, two years since, the white man had not disturbed the peaceful denizen of the forest; but within that period civilization has taken possession, and the beautiful prairies have been converted into broad fields, yielding bountifully, thus enriching the farmer, and converting a wide solitude into a settled district, numbering nearly or quite 5,000 inhabitants. The same is true, not only of other localities in this district, but of the entire southern portion of the Territory.

Quite a number of mills are already in operation in different parts of the district, and many more are in process of construction. Many thriving towns are springing up in the interior, and along the Minnesota Valley, among which are Stockton, St. Charles, Rochester, Mantorville, Faribault, Oronoco, Ashland, St. Peter, Traverse des Sioux, etc. Schools and churches are fast furnishing the means of mental and moral culture. A charter for a railroad has been obtained and accepted, to connect the Mississippi at Winona with the waters of the Minnesota River; and, when this shall be completed, the district will have unrivalled facilities of intercommunication.

Red Wing Land District.—Messrs. Phelps and Graham, in a recent communication to us, estimate that the population of the district has more than quadrupled during the past year, 1855. From the declaratory statements filed in that office, it would seem that that settlement has reached far back into the interior, and, in some instances, entire townships, with occasional exceptions, have been claimed by the pre-emptor. There is yet, however, in the district, a large quantity of very desirable farming land, unclaimed and unsettled, and which offers great inducements to the settler, from its accessibility, and the ease with which an excellent and permanent market can be reached.

The Mississippi skirts the district on the east, and the Minnesota, in the valley of which are the most beautiful and fertile lands in the West, runs twice diagonally across the district. The Cannon and Vermillion Rivers, with their branches, the branches of the Zumbro, and the smaller streams running into the Mississippi and Minnesota, afford excellent water power, and make this region of country the best watered in Minnesota.

Red Wing, Hastings, Shakopee, Henderson, and Le Sueur, among the most flourishing towns in the Territory, are in this district. Their growth, although marvellous, has scarcely equalled the growth of the back country which supports them. Under the operation of the pre-emption law, the country, for one so entirely new, is settling densely, and where, a year ago, there was scarcely a habitation, are now to be seen towns and farming settlements, which, for extent of improvements and appearance of prosperity, will find no parallel in the settlement of the West.

The settlers of this district are a pretty general admixture of the natives of the States, Germans, Irish, Swedes, Norwegians, etc.; the native-born population, however, largely predominating over all classes. The settlers are enterprising, industrious and prosperous.

The Red Wing district is eminently an agricultural one. The back country is undulating, with numerous streams. It is mainly prairie, interspersed with groves of trees, and backed by the "Big Woods," with its inexhaustible supply of the choicest timber. There are also many charming lakes scattered over the district. This district is situated north of the Winona and south of the Minneapolis district. The office is located at Red Wing, the county-seat of Goodhue county. The district is thirty miles wide, and runs west to the Big Sioux.

New Land Districts.—The recent session of Congress passed a bill, providing "That all that

portion of the Territory of Minnesota which lies north of the line dividing townships 45 and 46, north of the base line east of the Mississippi River, and north of the nearest township line, to be determined hereafter by the commissioner of the general land office, west of said river, extending thence west to the Missouri River, be, and the same is hereby, divided into and shall constitute two additional land districts, to wit: All that portion lying east of the line dividing ranges 18 and 19, west of the fourth principal meridian, shall constitute a land district, to be called the northeastern land district; and all that portion west of the line dividing said ranges 18 and 19 shall constitute an additional land district in said Territory, to be called the northwestern land district—the location of the offices for which shall be designated by the President of the United States, and shall by him from time to time be changed, as the public interests may seem to require."

An appropriation of $40,000 for the survey of the same has also been made, said surveys to show meridian, standard, parallel, township, and section lines.

The land office for one of the above districts will be upon the north shore of Lake Superior; the other on the Mississippi River, near Sandy Lake, or between the Mississippi and the Red River of the North. *So all this immense country is now subject to settlement!*

PRE-EMPTION LAW. — We give below the points which persons wishing to make pre-emptions are required to observe, for the satisfaction of the officers at the different land offices:

1. The settler must never before have had the benefit of pre-emption under the act.

2. He must not, at the time of making the pre-emption, be the owner of three hundred and twenty acres of land in any State or Territory in the United States.

3. He must settle upon and improve the land, in good faith, for his own exclusive use or benefit, and not with the intention of selling it on speculation; and must not make, directly or indirectly, any contract or agreement, in any way or manner, with any person or persons, by which the title which he may acquire from the United States should inure, in whole or in part, to the benefit of anybody but himself.

4. He must be twenty-one years of age and a citizen of the United States; or, if a foreigner, must have declared his intention to become a citizen before the proper authority, and received a certificate to that effect.

5. He must build a house on the land, live in it, and make it his exclusive home, and must be an inhabitant of the same at the time of making application for pre-emption. (Until lately, a single man might board with his nearest neighbor; but the same is now required of a single as a married

man, except that if married the family of the settler must also live in the house.)

6. The law requires that more or less improvement be made on the land, such as breaking, fencing, etc.; but pre-emptions are granted where a half-acre is broken and inclosed.

7. It is necessary that no other person entitled to the right of pre-emption reside on the land at the same time.

8. No person is permitted to remove from his own land and make a pre-emption in the same State or Territory.

9. The settler is required to bring with him to the land office a written or printed application, setting forth the facts in his case of the first, second, and third requirement here mentioned, with a certificate appended, to be signed by the register and receiver; and make affidavit to the same.

10. He is also required to bring with him a respectable witness of his acquaintance, who is knowing to the facts of his settlement, to make affidavit to the fourth, fifth, sixth, seventh, and eighth requirements here mentioned, with the same set forth on paper, with a corresponding blank certificate attached, to be signed by the land officers.

11. The pre-emptor, if a foreigner, must bring with him to the land office duplicates of his naturalization papers, duly signed by the official from whom they were received.

12. A minor, who is the head of a family, or a

widow, may also pre-empt; their families being required to live on the land. The settler is requested to file a written declaratory statement of his intention to pre-empt, before he can proceed with his pre-emption.

Fees. — 1st. The fee required by the register, for filling a declaratory statement, is one dollar. 2d. For granting a pre-emption, the register and receiver can receive fifty cents. 3d. For duplicate of the map of any township, one dollar is required by the register.

There is nothing in this law to prevent a single unmarried woman from pre-empting, providing she be the "head of a family." The settler must file his declaratory statement within three months from the time of commencing his improvements. After filing his declaratory statement, the claimant can 'prove up" his claim any time within one year, if the lands are in market; if not, he can defer payment till the lands come into market.

It may not be out of place here to allude to the ease with which the soil can be brought into cultivation, and the rich harvests it yields, in comparison with the amount of labor expended. A farm can be opened on the prairie, and enough raised in a single summer to pay for it. In the woodland, the process is more tedious, and, at first, not so profitable; but it is generally conceded that, in the end, a farm in the woodland will be more desirable than one on the prairie, as the soil is thought to be stronger and better adapted to wheat, fruit, etc. Emigrants from timbered countries generally locate in the woodland, while those from the prairie regions of Illinois, Iowa, and Wisconsin settle on the prairies here.

The cost of clearing and fencing the timbered land ranges from $18 to $30 per acre. The cost of breaking up the prairie is from $4.50 to $7 per acre. The first crop is put in on the sod, and is generally very good. Oats and corn do very well when they are raised in this way, as do also potatoes, pumpkins, melons, and all kinds of vegetables.

CHAPTER XIX.

TERRITORIAL ROADS THROUGH MINNESOTA. — RAILROADS. — THE LUMBER BUSINESS.

CONGRESS has made liberal appropriations for roads and public improvements in the Territory, with the aid of which, and through the enterprise of the people, there are now good roads between all the important points in the Territory. The Territorial road from St. Paul to Sioux City, on the Missouri, is completed to Mankato, and passable its entire length. The last session of Congress appropriated $50,000 for a wagon road from Fort Ridgely to the South Pass in the Rocky Mountains. There are already good roads between St. Paul and the Fort.

RAILROADS TO AND THROUGH MINNESOTA. — Inasmuch as a diversity of opinion exists among the citizens of the several more important towns, as to which of the numerous railroad routes projected thither is of greatest importance to the Territory, the question was submitted to Governor Gorman, whose reply follows:

EXECUTIVE OFFICE, MINNESOTA TERRITORY,
St. Paul, July 22, 1856.

N. H. PARKER, ESQ.

SIR, — I have received yours, desiring to have my opinion as to the importance of railroad routes in Minnesota. In reply, I have to say, that every person may have their own views about where railroads should first be located; but I have no hesitation in saying, that a road from Chicago through Wisconsin to St. Paul would be most beneficial to this capital and its vicinity, and such a road is now proposed. Chartered companies have been organized, and a grant of land made by Congress to the State of Wisconsin for that object.

A grant of land will most probably be made for a road from Winona on the Mississippi River to St. Peters on the Minnesota River, and a road from St. Paul to St. Peters, on the Minnesota River; also one from the Iowa line to St. Paul, and thence to Lake Superior. One of the Iowa roads is also pointing to St. Peters, which is twelve miles below Mankato; and St. Peters is perhaps the most flourishing point on that river. Whatever road reaches St. Peters first will command, for many years, the trade of that lovely valley of the Minnesota River, which is the Nile of our Territory, unsurpassed in any part of the Northwest.

If Wisconsin pushes a road there first, she will command the trade of all southern Minnesota. If Iowa taps it first by any road, she will command it; and it is not to be disguised that this valley is to be the most populous part of this Territory and future State.

The capital of this State will probably go to St. Peters, especially as so many railroads are pointing there. The grants of land for these roads will be made by this Congress at their present session. The bill has passed the committee on public lands, and ordered to be introduced, as I have before indicated. I trust this may be useful to you, and through you, to the country.

Respectfully, W. A. GORMAN.

THE MINNESOTA PINERIES.— THE LUMBERING BUSINESS. — Of the area of the pine region of

Minnesota there are no reliable data accessible; but that the lumbering business is one of the most important and profitable to the Territory, none can question who will examine the statistics. An estimate was made last spring, by a gentleman well versed in the affairs of the pineries, of the number of feet of logs that would probably be floated down from the pineries during the last spring. His estimates were: "From Rum River, 120,000,000; from the Mississippi, 40,000,000; from the St. Croix, 160,000,000; from the Chippewa, 75,000,000; total, 395,000,000."

These figures may look large to one not acquainted with the extent of the business; but the following, from the Prescott Transcript, dated in June, will show the estimate to be within bounds. Port Prescott is at the mouth of St. Croix Lake, a favorable stand-point. It says: "Twenty-six rafts of logs have been floated out of the St. Croix within the past week. These rafts, we are informed by a reliable lumberman, will make from twelve to fifteen hundred thousand feet of lumber each; making in all over thirty million feet, or $600,000 worth. That will do for one week! The estimate of one hundred and fifty million for the St. Croix, this season, may be safely multiplied by two. There is more lumber floating this season than in any one of the past four years."

To this article the St. Croix Union, published at Stillwater, adds: "We presume every word of the above is strictly true. Rafts are leaving Stillwater for the southern market almost every day; and, as soon as they leave, others float down from the boom, and take their places. From $75,000 to $125,000 worth of logs may be seen, any day, in the lake opposite Stillwater; and this has been true for the four or five weeks just past. The amount of capital invested here in the lumber business amounts to nearly two millions of dollars.

From an article on Stillwater, by the editor of the Minnesotian, I extract the following:

" Stillwater, it is well known, is the head-quarters of the lumber trade of the St. Croix; and, as that trade has extended this year to more than twice its former figure, of course Stillwater materially prospers accordingly. Since the opening of navigation, pine logs and lumber have been measured by the acre at the bend of Lake St. Croix and on the river above. Three or four thousand men have found constant employment in getting the logs ready for market, and transporting them thereto. The great bulk of the trade is over for the season, yet logs and rafts still line the shore of the lake, and cover its surface from its head to a considerable distance below Hudson. The amount of lumber produced on the St. Croix, which has been and will be sent out this season, is over two hundred million feet. Logs still bring a very high price below; and of course this business is bound to go on increasing from year to year.

"LUMBER MANUFACTURING AT STILLWATER.—Stillwater has now four extensive saw-mills—the old McKusick mills, driven by water power; and Sawyer & Heaton's, Hersey, Staples & Co.'s, and Schulenberg's steam-mills. The two latter are considered the best mills in the Territory—Hersey, Staples & Co.'s being the most extensive of the two. It is, perhaps, the finest working mill in the West, and is in all departments as near perfection as machinery can be brought by human skill. It works three upwright saws and a gang; also, flooring and siding circular saws, and lath machines. The flooring saws are rigged to *cut both ways*, thus saving half the time usually consumed in operating machines of this kind. Everything about the mill is done by machinery, even to the filing of saws, the handling and shifting of lumber, and the removal of slabs. Mr. Staples' lumber is extensively used in St. Paul, and is pronounced by our builders to be much the best in use here, both in regard to quality and manufacture. The mill is capable of cutting one hundred and twenty-five thousand feet in twenty-four hours."

Further items respecting the lumbering regions, and of vacant lands therein, will be found in chapter XVIII. of this work.

CHAPTER XX.

SCHOOLS AND CHURCHES.

No portion of the United States has more liberal appropriations for educational purposes than Minnesota. Every sixteenth and thirty-sixth section in every township is reserved and set apart for the support of common schools. This land is not available for the support of schools until Minnesota shall become a State, which will probably be during the next session of Congress; as it is certain she has now within her Territory more than enough inhabitants to entitle her to be admitted. In travelling over the Territory, I found schools in almost every town and village. There is a scarcity of female teachers; as men can make from two to three dollars per day at out-door employments, which, in this healthy latitude, they much prefer, this branch will be left almost entirely to females.

The Hamlin University, at Red Wing, is a chartered institution, with donations sufficient to erect a commodious college edifice. The preparatory department has an attendance of some seventy scholars, and is ably conducted.

The University of Minnesota was incorporated by Congress in 1851, and located at St. Anthony. The incorporation act provides that "the proceeds of all lands that may hereafter be granted by the United States to the Territory, for the support of a university, shall be and remain a perpetual fund, to be called 'the university fund,' the interest of which shall be appropriated to the support of a university." From the proceedings of a meeting of the regents, held on the 26th May, I notice that property which cost the university $5,500 is now worth $20,000. In addition to this, the university owns forty-three thousand acres of land, which, at the moderate estimate of $10 an acre, would be worth $430,000. This property, with careful management, will in a few years be worth over a million of dollars; which leaves no room for a doubt that the University of Minnesota will be one of the most wealthy institutions in the United States.

It is to be hoped that the regents will keep a good look-out for the interests of the university, and that its officers may prove more faithful and trusty than one who made a $200,000 mistake in his own favor in an adjoining State.

A university is about being organized on the Minnesota River; but at what point, I did not learn. All the larger towns and cities in the Territory are erecting large and substantial district school-houses.

Of churches, it need only be stated that nearly all the Orthodox denominations have regularly organized societies in the larger places, and that, in smaller towns and neighborhoods, the denomination which predominates leads in the organization of a church. There seems to be much unity and harmony among the different churches. The primary convention of the Protestant Episcopal Church met in St. Paul, on the 1st of May, when a permanent organization was effected, and "the diocese of Minnesota," created.

The fifth annual meeting of the Minnesota Bible Society was held in St. Paul, on the 27th of April. There are in the Territory sixteen county societies, all auxiliary to the parent society. The total distribution of books during the year amounted to $646. Each of the hotels, as also the boats plying the northern waters, have been supplied by this society with the Bible. Who can estimate the benefits upon the community, and upon individuals, conferred by the labors of this association?

CHAPTER XXI.

THE INDIAN TRIBES OF THE NORTHWEST. — FEDERAL, LAND, TERRITORIAL, AND DISTRICT OFFICERS. — INDIAN AGENTS. — NEWSPAPERS. — TABLE OF DISTANCES.

The author collected numerous matters of interest respecting the Indians of the northwest. Finding the particulars too extensive for this volume, he will merely mention the names of the principal tribes in the Territory. A volume is in course of preparation, giving a full account of the condition of the Indians, their costumes, habits, and dialects, their legends and mythologies.

The Indians that formerly occupied Illinois, Wisconsin, and Iowa, have been removed to Minnesota, and there are now in the Territory about forty thousand, who may be thus classified:

Medawakantwan (Sioux) or Dacotah. — Red Wing band, 300; Kaposia band, 400; Black-dog band, 300; Lake Calhoun band, 250; Good-road's band, 300; Little Six's band, 400.

Wahpetonwans (Sioux). — Little Rapids band, 150; Lac-Qui-Parle band, 400; Big Stone Lake band, 150.

Sissitons. — Traverse des Sioux band, 350; Little-rock band, 300; Lac Traverse band, 350; besides these, there are some 400 more, unorganized.

The *Wahpekootays* number perhaps 300.

Yauktons. — The Cut-Heads number about 100; the Who-do-not-eat-buffalo-cows band, 100; People-of-the-poles band, 100.

Tetons. — The Ogolawla band, 300; the Sioune band, 150.

The *Chippeway* or *Ojibway* nation are the most intelligent and the most chivalric. We have more full accounts of the dialects, legends, mythological history, etc., of this tribe than of any other in the country. They number about 8000.

The first Indian reservation reached by the traveller is that of the Winnebagoes, on the Blue Earth River, consisting of two hundred and seven thousand three hundred and sixty acres, or eighteen miles square, of land. This reserve is under the control of Colonel J. E. Fletcher, agent of the Winnebagoes, of whom there are about 2000. From Colonel F., I gathered the following statistics, which will convey some idea of the provisions made for the Indians. The Sissitons, and some other tribes, however, report themselves as suffering for want of food and raiment. The appropriations to the Winnebagoes are: money, $48,000; goods, $20,000; provisions, $10,000; salt, barrels, 50; tobacco, pounds, 45,000; education, $6,300; agriculture, $3,365; general improvement, $4,250 medicine and attendance, $1000; salary of miller, $600. Three blacksmith's shops are also supported for their benefit. By the treaty of 1846, $10,000 was appropriated for the establishment of manual labor schools, which object has never yet been effected.

Persons wishing to visit this reserve will stop at Mankato, where they will be correctly directed to the Agency, twelve miles distant.

FEDERAL OFFICERS LOCATED IN MINNESOTA.

Willis A. Gorman, Governor, St. Paul.
J. Travis Rosser, Secretary, "
W. H. Welch, Chief Justice, Red Wing.
A. G. Chatfield, Associate Justice, Belle Plain
Moses Sherburne, " " St. Paul.
M. W. Irwin, Marshal, St. Paul.
Norman Eddy, District Attorney, St. Paul.

LAND OFFICERS.

T. M. Fullerton, Register, Stillwater.
Wm. Holcombe, Receiver, "
G. W. Sweet, Register, Sauk Rapids.
W. H. Wood, Receiver, "
M. L. Olds, Register, Minnneapolis.
R. P. Russell, Receiver, "
W. W. Phelps, Register, Red Wing.
C. Graham, Receiver, "
D. Upham, Register, Winona.
L. D. Smith, Receiver, "
Major Bennett, Register, Brownsville.
J. H. McKinney, Receiver, "

INDIAN AGENTS.

J. E. Fletcher, Winnebago Agency.
J. B. Herriman, Chippeway "
R. G. Murphy, Sioux "

TERRITORIAL OFFICERS.

H. M. Rice, Delegate in Congress, Washington, D. C.
J. R. Brown, Territorial Printer, Henderson.
L. Emmett, Attorney General, St. Paul.
C. E. Leonard, Treasurer, St. Anthony.
Julius Geoegh, Auditor, St. Paul.
Wm. Sprigg Hall, Superintendent of Common Schools, St. Paul.

DISTRICT OFFICERS.

Robert Hastie, Surveyor of Lumber, Stillwater.
D. Stanchfield, " " St. Anthony.
W. Lauver, " " Red Wing.

NEWSPAPERS IN MINNESOTA.

Name.		Location.
Pioneer and Democrat,	Daily,	St. Paul.
St. Paul Daily Times,	"	"
St. Paul Daily Free Press,	"	"
The Daily Minnesotian,	"	"
St. Paul Advertiser,	Monthly,	"
St. Croix Union,	Weekly,	Stillwater.
St. Anthony Express,	"	St. Anthony.
St. Anthony Republican,	"	"
North-Western Democrat,	"	"
Sauk Rapids Frontierman,	"	Sauk Rapids.
St. Peter Weekly Courier,	"	St. Peter.
Shakopee Independent,	"	Shakopee.
Red Wing Sentinel,	"	Red Wing.
Winona Republican,	"	Winona.
Winona Argus,	"	"
Brownsville Herald,	"	Brownsville.

Chatfield Democrat,	Weekly,	Chatfield.
Preston Journal,	"	Preston.
Stillwater Republican,	"	Stillwater.
St. Cloud Democrat,	"	St. Cloud.
Henderson Democrat,	"	Henderson.
Minnesota Gazette,	"	Red Wing.
Dacotah Journal,	"	Hastings.
Wabashaw Journal,	"	Wabashaw.

[NOTE. — The author returns thanks to the Press generally, for numerous favors. If they will forward copies of their papers containing important territorial or local information, to him, at Clinton, Iowa, he will be enabled to post up more fully on their several localities, in future editions.]

TABLE OF DISTANCES.

RIVER DISTANCES.

MISSISSIPPI RIVER.

From St. Louis to Rock Island.	Miles.
Alton,	22
Grafton,	18
Milan,	24
Wiota,	42
Worthington,	52
Westport,	57
Hamburg,	62
Clarksville,	80
Louisiana,	82
Scott's Landing,	97
Cincinnati,	105
Saverton,	115
Hannibal,	123
Marion City,	133
Quincy,	143
La Grange,	155
Smoot's Landing,	159
Canton,	161
Tully,	163
Gregory's Landing,	175
Alexandria,	185
Keokuk,	190
Nashville,	198
Montrose,	202
Nauvoo,	204
Fort Madison,	214
Pontoosuc,	220
Burlington,	235
Oquawka,	250
Keithsburg,	262
New Boston,	269
Muscatine,	299
Drury,	304
Salem,	309
Buffalo and Andalusia,	321
Rock Island and Davenport,	334

ROCK ISLAND TO GALENA.

From Rock Island to		Miles.
Moline,	3	
Hampton,	9	12

From Rock Island to		Miles.
Le Claire and Pt. Byron,	6	18
Princeton,	5	23
Cordovia,	1	24
Camanche,	10	34
Albany,	2	36
Clinton,	7	43
Fulton,	1	44
Lyons,	1	45
Sabula,	15	60
Savanna,	2	62
Bellevue,	18	80
Galena,	12	92

GALENA TO ST. PAUL.

From Galena to		Miles.
Dubuque,	24	
Dunleith,	1	25
Potosi Landing,	14	39
Waupaton,	10	49
Buena Vista,	5	54
Cassville,	4	58
Gutenberg,	10	68
Clayton,	12	80
Wyalusing,	5	85
McGregor's,	6	91
Prairie du Chien,	4	95
Red House,	5	100
Johnson's Landing,	2	102
Lafayette,	30	132
Columbus,	2	134
Lansing,	1	135
De Soto,	6	141
Victory,	10	151
Badaxe City,	10	161
Warner's Landing,	6	167
Brownsville,	10	177
La Crosse,	12	189
Dacotah,	12	201
Richmond,	6	207
Monteville,	5	212
Homer,	10	222
Winona,	7	229
Fountain City,	12	241
Mount Vernon,	14	255
Minneiska,	4	259
Alma,	15	274
Wabashaw,	10	284
Nelson's Landing,	3	287
Reed's Landing,	2	289
Foot of Lake Pepin,	2	291
North Pepin,	6	297
Johnstown,	2	299
Lake City,	5	304
Central Point,	2	306
Florence,	3	309
Maiden Rock,	3	312
Westerville,	3	315
Wacouta (head of lake),	12	327
Red Wing,	6	333
Thing's Landing,	7	340
Diamond Bluff,	8	348
Prescott,	13	361
Point Douglas,	1	362
Hastings,	3	365
Gray Cloud,	12	377
Pine Bend,	4	381
Red Rock,	8	389
Kaposia,	3	392
St. Paul,	5	397

PRESCOTT TO THE FALLS OF ST. CROIX.

From Falls St. Croix to		
Afton,	14	
Hudson,	8	22
Stillwater.	8	30
Arcola Mills,	8	38
Marine,	5	43
Osceola,	20	63
Falls St. Croix,	14	77

ST. PAUL TO YELLOW MEDICINE.

From St. Paul to	By River.	
Mendota,	6	
Fort Snelling,	1	7
Oak Grove,	10	17
Credit River,	4	21

From St. Paul to	Miles. By River.		By Land.
Bloomington,	7	28	
Hennepin,	5	33	
Shakopee,	8	41	25½
Yorkville,	2	43	
Chaska,	3	46	
Carver,	3	49	
Louisville,	1	50	
Little Rapids,	4	54	
San Francisco,		54	
Sand Prairie,	5	59	
Bristol Landing,	8	67	
Belle Plain,	5	72	45
Roberts' Landing,	3	75	
Swan Landing,	3	78	
Russell's Landing,	2	80	
Walker's Landing,	2	82	
Albright's Landing,	1	83	
Donohan's Landing,	4	87	
Henderson,	14	99	55
Le Sueur,	12	111	
Traverse,	18	129	68
St. Peter,	5	134	69
Kasota,	4	138	
Mankato,	30	169	76
South Bend,	7	176	80
Eureka,	28	204	
Cottonwood River,	50	254	
New Ulm,	22	276	
Little Rock,	40	316	
Fort Ridgley,	20	336	
Redwood,	30	366	
Yellow Medicine,	80	446	

St. Paul to Lake Superior.

From St. Paul to	Miles.	
St. Anthony,	9	
Rice Creek,	7	16
St. Francis or Rum Riv.,	9	25
Itasca,	7	32
Elk River,	6	38
Big Lake,	10	48
Big Meadow (Sturgis),	18	66
Benton City (Sauk Rapids),	10	76
Watab,	6	82
Little Rock,	2	84
Platte River,	12	96
Swan River,	10	106
Little Falls,	3	109
Belle Prairie,	5	114
Fort Ripley,	10	124
Crow Wing River,	6	130
Sandy Lake,	120	250
Savanah Portage,	15	265
Across the Portage,	5	270
Down Savanah River to St. Louis River,	20	290
Fon du Lac,	60	350
Lake Superior,	22	372

St. Paul to Fon du Lac.

From St. Paul to		
Stillwater,	18	
Arcola,	5	23
Marine Mills,	6	29
Falls St. Croix,	19	48
Porkagema,	40	88
Fon du Lac,	75	164

St. Paul to Pembina.

From St. Paul to		
Crow Wing River,	130	
Otter Tail Lake,	70	200
Rice River,	74	274
Sand Hills River,	70	340
Grand Fork, Red River,	40	380
Pembina,	80	460

Via the Lakes.

Sandy Lake,	250	
Leech Lake,	150	400
Red Lake,	80	480
Pembina,	150	630

From St. Paul, East.

From St. Paul to	
Stillwater,	18

From St. Paul to		Miles.
Hudson, ...		29
New York, . .		1700
Washington City, . .		1924

SHAKOPEE TO SIOUX AGENCY.

From Shakopee to		
Henderson, . . .	29	74
Fort Ridgley, .	45	74
Sioux Agency, .	12	86

TO GLENCOE.

Chaska, ...	3¼	
Carver City, .	2½	6
San Francisco, .	4	10
Glencoe, . .	25	35

TO GREENWOOD.

Lake Minnewashta,	6½	
Minnetouka Narrows,	3½	10
Tazaska, . .	1	11
Pioneer creek, .	6	17
Greenwood, .	6	23

MINNETOUKA CITY.

Chanhassen P. O. .	5	
Excelsior, . .	3	8
St. Albans, . .	1	9
Minnetouka city,	6	15

TO CEDAR LAKE.

Spring Lake, .	6½	
Cedar Lake, . .	7½	14

TO FARIBAULT.

Credit River, .	9	
Lakeville, . .	10	19
Faribault, .	22	41

APPENDIX.

SIXTH SESSION OF THE MINNESOTA LEGISLATURE.

The sixth session of the Minnesota Legislature commenced on Wednesday, January 3d, 1855, at the capitol, in St. Paul. The following is a list of the members, their places of residence and occupations:

COUNCILLORS.

Name.	No. District.	Residence.	Occupation.
J. E. Mower,	1	Arcola.	Mill Owner.
Albert Stimson,	1	Stillwater.	Lumberman.
Isaac Van Etten,	2	St. Paul.	Lawyer.
Wm. P. Murray,	2	St. Paul.	Lawyer.
C. T. Stearns,	3	St. Anthony.	Cabinet Maker.
Wm. Freeborn,	4	Red Wing.	Merchant.
S. B. Olmstead,	5	Fort Ripley.	Farmer.
J. R. Brown,	6	Henderson.	Merchant.
N. W. Kittson,	7	Pembina.	Indian Trader.

REPRESENTATIVES.

Names.	No. District.	Residence.	Occupation.
F. Andros,	5	Long Prairie.	Physician.
James Bealty,	5	Itasca.	Farmer.
D. F. Brawley,	2	St. Paul.	Brick Maker.
C. S. Cave,	2	St. Paul.	Grocer.
Wm. Davis,	2	St. Paul.	S.B. Engineer.

J. B. Dixon,	1	Stillwater.	Printer.
A. M. Fridley,	3	St. Anthony.	Sheriff.
Chas. Grant,	7	Pembina.	Indian Trader.
Reuben Haus,	2	St. Paul.	Carpenter.
D. M. Hanson,	6	Minneapolis.	Lawyer.
Joseph Le May,	2	St. Paul.	Justice Peace.
J. S. Norris,	1	Cottage Grove.	Farmer.
S. B. Regester,	1	Taylor's Falls.	Lumberman.
Joseph Rolette,	7	Pembina.	Indian Trader.
H. H. Sibley,	6	Mendota.	Indian Trader.
D. Stanchfield,	3	St. Anthony.	Lumberman.
Wm. Thompson,	4	Brownsville.	Mill Owner.
Wm. Willim,	1	Stillwater.	Plasterer.

The Council was permanently organized by the selection of Hon. S. B. OLMSTEAD, of Benton county, as President (who resigned his seat at the end of the session, and Hon. W. P. MURRAY was elected in his place), and A. J. MORGAN, Esq., of St. Paul, Secretary.

The House chose JAMES S. NORRIS, of Cottage Grove, Washington county, Speaker; and for Clerk, elected J. C. SHEPLEY, of St. Anthony.

The Legislature remained in session sixty days, adjourning on the 4th of March. The following is a list of the acts, joint resolutions, and memorials passed during the session.

GENERAL LAWS AND CHARTERS, OTHER THAN FERRY.

A bill to define the boundaries of certain counties.

An act to change the name of Ann Elizabeth White to Ann Elizabeth Tinker.

A bill to provide for laying out certain Territorial roads.

An act legalizing the town of Winona, and for other purposes.

[A mechanic lien law was added to this bill—it allows mechanics a lien for their services on houses and other property.]

A bill to change the time of holding courts in Ramsey county.

An act for the benefit of common schools of the Territory, and for other purposes.

[This bill is to protect lumber in booms, and provides penalties in fines, for violations of the law, which go to the benefit of the common schools of the Territory.]

An act to provide for the appointment of a commissioner of emigration for the Territory of Minnesota.

An act to locate a Territorial road from St. Augusta, on the Mississippi river, to Lac Traverse.

A bill for a line of telegraph from St. Paul to St. Anthony and Minneapolis.

A bill for an act allowing a change of venue in certain cases, and for other purposes.

[This act also amended the revised statutes, giving the courts greater powers than they now exercise in divorce cases.]

An act to incorporate the German Reading Society of St. Cloud.

A bill to incorporate the Boston and Minnesota Mining Company.

An act to incorporate the St. Joseph's Hospital.

A bill to provide for the improvement of the Minnesota river.

An act to incorporate the Lake Pepin Boom Company.

A bill for an act to incorporate the Monticello Academy at Monticello.

An act to incorporate the Territorial Emigration Society.

An act to incorporate the Minnesota Typographical Union.

An act to incorporate the Sisters of Propagation of Faith Society, of St. Joseph, at Pembina.

An act to authorize the construction of a dam across Crow river.

An act to incorporate the Pioneer Hook and Ladder Company of St. Paul.

An act relative to the county-seat of Houston county.

A bill to amend an act, entitled an act to incorporate the Minnesota Western Railroad Company.

A bill to confirm the qualifications of certain county officers in Sibley county.

An act prescribing rules and regulations for the execution of the trusts arising under the act of Congress, entitled, "An act for the relief of citizens of towns upon lands of the United States, under certain circumstances."

A bill to incorporate the Transit Railroad Company.

An act to incorporate the Pittsburg and Minnesota Mining Company, and for other purposes.

[This act located the county-seat of Carver county at San Francisco.]

A bill to locate the county-seat of Le Sueur county.

An act to restore to Ephraim H. Whittaker, his civil rights as a citizen of the United States.

An act to provide for laying out certain Territorial Roads in Minnesota Territory.

A bill to provide for laying out a Territorial road from St. Paul to Elliota.

An act to incorporate the city of Stillwater, in the county of Washington.

An act to incorporate the Root River Valley and Southern Minnesota Railroad Company, and for other purposes.

[This bill located the county-seat of Fillmore county at Carimona, and of Wright county at Monticello.]

An act to amend an act entitled, "An act to incorporate the St. Croix Boom Company."

An act to incorporate the town of Henderson, and for other purposes.

An act to incorporate the city of St. Anthony.

An act to amend an act entitled, "An act to incorporate the St. Anthony Boom Company," approved March 27th, 1852.

A bill to provide for the apportionment of members of the Legislative Assembly of the Territory of Minnesota.

A bill to amend an act entitled, "An act relating to auctioneers."

An act to organize the county of Stearns, and for other purposes.

[This bill also located the county-seat of Stearns county at St. Cloud; and provided for the removal of county officers in case they should refuse to keep their offices at the county-seat of their respective counties.]

A bill to amend an act entitled, "An act to incorporate the Minnesota Western Railroad Company."

An act supplementary to an act entitled, "An act to amend the Minnesota Western Railroad Company."

An act providing that copies of the records in the office of Register of Deeds may be admissible in evidence.

A bill for an act to locate a Territorial road from St. Cloud to intersect the old Red river road of the North.

An act entitled, an act to incorporate the city of St. Paul, Ramsey county.

An act to provide for taking a census of the population of this Territory.

An act to abolish imprisonment for debt and for other purposes.

An act to provide for the election of Supervisors of Roads, and for other purposes.

An act to defray the expenses of the Legislative Assembly of Minnesota Territory.

FERRY CHARTERS.

An act to amend an act granting to James M. Goodhue and Isaac N. Goodhue the right to establish and maintain a ferry across the Mississippi river.

An act granting to Samuel H. McManus, Wm. Creighton, and James C. Beekman, the right to establish and maintain a ferry across the Mississippi river.

A bill to amend an act granting to Daniel F. Brawley the right to establish and maintain a ferry across the Mississippi river.

A bill granting to William L. Ames, George Hezlep, George W. Farrington, C. H. Parker, and William B. Dodd, the right to establish and maintain a ferry across the Minnesota river.

An act granting to O. H. Kelley the right to establish and maintain a ferry across the Mississippi river.

A bill granting to Moses Perrin and Joseph H. Taylor the right to establish and maintain a ferry across Lake St. Croix.

An act granting to George R. Stuntz the right to establish and maintain a ferry across the St. Louis river.

An act granting to Wm. H. Oliver the right to establish and maintain a ferry across Lake St. Croix.

An act granting to Ira Myrick the right to establish and maintain a ferry across the Minnesota river, at Le Sueur city.

An act granting to John Hamilton the right to establish and maintain a ferry across the St. Croix river.

An act granting to Lewis Stone, A. C. Riggs, George Houghton, and H. N. Corbett, the right to establish and maintain a ferry across the Mississippi river.

An act granting to Wm. Foster the right to establish and maintain a ferry across the Minnesota river, at San Francisco, in Carver county.

An act granting to Orrin W. Rice the right to establish and maintain a ferry across the head of the Bay of Superior.

An act to incorporate the Winona Ferry Company.

An act granting to John L. Wilson, Anton Edelbrock, and Wm. A. Corbett, the right to establish and maintain a ferry across the Mississippi river, at St. Cloud, and for other purposes.

[The "other purposes" granted to Antoine Roberts a ferry charter across the Minnesota river, in Le Sueur county.]

An act granting to W. W. Sweeney, William Louver, Richard Freeborn, and Norris Hobart, the right to establish and maintain a ferry across the Mississippi river.

An act granting to Carmi P. Garlick the right to establish and maintain a ferry across the St. Croix river.

An act granting to O. W. Streeter the right to establish and maintain a ferry across the Mississippi river.

MEMORIALS TO CONGRESS.

For $10,000 for the completion of the Mendota and Wabashaw road.

For $5,000 for the construction of a Territorial road from the west bank of the Mississippi river, opposite the lower portion of the city of St. Paul, to intersect the Territorial road now being constructed from Mendota to Wabashaw.

For $5,000 to extend the Mendota and Big Sioux river road from Mendota to the west bank of the Mississippi, opposite the city of St. Paul.

For $10,000 for the construction of a military road from Fort Ripley to or near the mouth of Pembina river.

For an appropriation to complete the government works at Fort Ridgley.

For an appropriation in Minnesota Territory, for the improvement of the navigation of the Mississippi river.

For an appropriation for the construction of a military road from Fort Ridgley, to connect with the Mendota and Big Sioux road.

JOINT RESOLUTIONS.

A joint resolution relative to a change in the Distributing Post-office from Dubuque to Galena.

Relative to an error in the charge of $33.17 to the county of Washington, by the Territorial treasurer, in the year 1850.

Relative to the binding of the journals.

The above list of acts comprises several general laws of great importance to the people of the Territory—among them may be ranked the apportionment bill, an act defining the boundaries of certain counties, for the abolishment of imprisonment for debt, etc.

The bill defining the boundaries of certain counties, provides for the erection of the following new counties: Olmstead, Dodge, Mower, Freeborn, Faribault, Steele, Carver, Renville, Davis, Wright, Stearns, Brown, Newton, Todd, Itasca, and Superior.

The apportionment bill is a measure designed to give the people of the Territory, west of the Mississippi, a fair representation in the Territorial Legislature. By it, the number of members of the House is increased to thirty-eight, and of the Council to fifteen. A census of the Territory is to be taken in August, and, in the month following, a committee, composed of members of the two branches of the last Legislature, will meet in St. Paul, and determine the representation to which each Council district is entitled in the next Legislature. This committee is composed of the following gentlemen: Messrs. J. B. Brown, Albert Stimson, D. M. Hanson, Wm. A. Davis, and C. S. Cave. Their duties are important, and the people of the Territory require at their hands a faithful, impartial, and just apportionment of the Territory.

The Legislature also passed a bill granting an extension of time to the Minnesota and Northwestern Railroad Company. The bill was vetoed by the Governor, but was subsequently passed over the Governor's veto, by a constitutional majority.

POST-OFFICES IN MINNESOTA.

Amoka,
Babcock's Landing,
Belle Plain,
Benton,
Bloomington,
Brownsville,
Cass Lake,
Chanhassen,
Chatfield,
Cottage Grove,
Crow Wing,
Eagle Bluff,
Elk River,
Elliota,
Excelsior,
Faribault,
Fort Ridgley,
Fort Ripley,
Fort Snelling,
Hastings,
Henderson,
Itasca,
Kasota,
Lac qui Parle,
Lakeland,
Lakeville,
Le Sueur,
Long Prairie,
Mankato,
Manomin,
Marine Mills,
Mendota,
Milton Mills,
Minneapolis,
Minnetonka,
Minnesota City,
Mt. Vernon,
Pembina,
Point Douglas,
Portland,
Red Lake,
Red Rock,
Red Wing,
Reed's Landing,
Sauk Rapids,
Saint Anthony,
Saint Joseph,
Saint Paul,
Sioux Agency,
Shakopee,
Stillwater,
Swan River,
Taylor's Falls,
Traverse des Sioux,
Wacoota,
Wabashaw,
Watab,
Waterford,
Winona.

The following post-office appointments have recently been made:

At Spring Grove, in Houston county, Embrick Rundson has been appointed postmaster, in place of James Smith, resigned.

At Maple Plain, Hennepin county, a post-office has been established, and Irvin Shrewsbury appointed postmaster.

At Eureka, Nicollet county, a post-office has been established, and John Henderson appointed postmaster.

At Hamilton, Houston county, a post-office has been established, and Charles Smith appointed postmaster.

At Wasioja, Dodge county, a post-office has been established, and Eli P. Waterman appointed postmaster.

At New Ulm, Brown county, a post-office has been established, and Anton Kaus appointed postmaster.

The postmaster general has ordered that the service on route No. 14,050, from Traverse de Sioux to Eureka, be extended to New Ulm; also, the establishment of a special mail route from St. Cloud, via Hanley, Mille Lac, and Twin Lakes, to Superior. G. F. Brott has received the contract for carrying the mails.

The following new post-offices have been established in this Territory:

At Twin Lakes, St. Louis county, G. W. Berry, postmaster.

At Grand Portage, Superior county, H. H. McCullough, postmaster.

At Centralia, Dakota county, H. P. Sweet, postmaster.

At Beaver Bay, Superior county, R. McLean, postmaster.

At Mille Lac, Pine county, M. Leadbetter, postmaster.

At French River, Superior county, H. Smith, postmaster.

At Grand Marie, Superior county, R. Godfrey, postmaster.

At Hanley, Chisago county, John Hanley, postmaster.

At Neenah, Stearns county, H. B. Johnston, postmaster.

IOWA AND MINNESOTA LAND AGENCY.

The author, since the issue of his former works, has had hundreds of applications for information respecting certain localities in the West: the price of land or of town lots, good openings for manufactories, or mills, stores, or mechanics, or laborers, extra speculations, etc. Convinced of the need of such an agency, he has in his recent tours so arranged with reliable persons in various quarters, that he will be enabled to give almost any information desired of the West with promptness. Letters of inquiry are of importance to the applicant only, and a correct reply costs both time and money; therefore those writing, hereafter, will inclose from $1 to $5, according to the information desired, and the expense to be incurred. Lands bought and sold in every county in Iowa and Minnesota; taxes paid, and a general agency business transacted.

Letters relative to business in Minnesota should be addressed to Nathan H. Parker, care of Snyder & McFarlane, Land Agents, Minneapolis, Minnesota; those relative to matters west of the Des Moines River, to Parker & Davis, Sioux City, Iowa. Letters pertaining to matters on and east of the Des Moines River to be addressed to

NATHAN H. PARKER,
Clinton, Iowa.

www.ingramcontent.com/pod-product-compliance
Lightning Source LLC
LaVergne TN
LVHW021404110826
845150LV00007B/1778

* 9 7 8 1 4 2 5 5 1 2 0 9 5 *